Memories of A Southern Country Boy

John Dave "Pete" Fuller

Memories of A Southern Country Boy
Copyright © 2023 by John Dave (Pete) Fuller

Library of Congress Control Number:	2023906509
ISBN-13: Paperback:	978-1-64749-897-9
Hardback:	978-1-64749-898-6
ePub:	978-1-64749-889-4

All rights reserved. No part of this publication may be reproduced, distributed, or transmitted in any form or by any means, including photocopying, recording, or other electronic or mechanical methods, without the prior written permission of the publisher or author, except in the case of brief quotations embodied in critical reviews and certain other noncommercial uses permitted by copyright law.

Although every precaution has been taken to verify the accuracy of the information contained herein, the author and publisher assume no responsibility for any errors or omissions. No liability is assumed for damages that may result from the use of information contained within.

Printed in the United States of America

GoTo Publish

GoToPublish LLC
1-888-337-1724
www.gotopublish.com
info@gotopublish.com

Table of Contents

The Honeymooners 1
Saturday Afternoon At The Movies 5
Dead Man's Curve 7
The Hospital Ward 9
My First Football Letter 11
The Good Ole Days 13
Where's The Bathroom? 16
O.M. Bratton (Mr. B.) 18
The Soapbox Derby And Mr. Spudnutt 22
Beginner Band 1951 25
School Clothes 1945 28
Saturday Night Baseball 30
Grammar School 32
Born On The Wrong Side Of The Blanket 35
Where Baby Calves Come From 37
The Bouncer (25 To 3 Fight) 39
Little Henry, Alias "Pete" 42
Hi Mom! 45
Dave Fuller 47
The Piano Problem 49
Air Raids 52
James Lee "Snokie" Mulder 54
Schoolyard Football 56
Jail Time For A Ten-Year-Old? 58
Blue Hornet Football 60
Dehorning Cows 62
Life In The Fast Lane 64
Country Marriage 66

The Day Dave Fuller Was Born
(As Told By Delmus Fuller) 68
Don't Mess With Ecie 70
Sloppin' Hogs 72
Me And Goat 74
Sears And Roebuck Taught Me How To Read 76
Just Any Ole Bottle Will Do! 77
Little Game Hunter 79
Driver's Education 80
Halloween Carnival 82
Gran-Daddy Hicks And Jail Time 85
Delmus And The Sign Post 87
Snakin' Logs 89
Trick And No Treat 90
Additional Writings 92
Above The Bright Blue 93
Dibble Dabble 94
Water Tag 95
Elizabeth And Butch 96
My Territory As A Four-Year-Old 97
Readin' Material 98
Gamblin' Game 99
The Conception And Early Life Of John David
Fuller, Jr., Alias "Pete" 100
The Sweetgum Tree Game 102
Shootin' Snipe 103
This Is Your Life 104
Aborted 107
Oh Sweet Butterfly 108
Picture References 109

THE HONEYMOONERS

John Dave (Pete) Fuller

I woke up early this Saturday morning. This was my wedding day. No church wedding. No preacher. In fact, no wedding. My bride and me were to be married in Columbus, Georgia, by a judge.

Now this was not a shotgun wedding. My bride of 15 was not pregnant. In fact, we had never slept together. We were both virgins, but people will talk, especially, middle-aged, gossipy women who don't have a lot to do but sit around and talk about old men, young folks, and the latest gossip.

"This marriage will never last."

So spoke the gossipy prophets of doom. My marriage was the star attraction this week, number one on the hit parade.

My bride was to meet me at my house at nine o'clock. My parents, her mother, little brother and sister would travel to Columbus. I was anxious to get the show on the road and as nervous as all get out.

I was ready to go, and when nine o'clock rolled around, nobody had arrived. I was beginning to get really nervous. Nine-fifteen. Still nobody. Finally, nine-twenty and my bride and her family drove up. They had forgotten her birth certificate and had to go back. We all greeted one another and everybody was ready to go.

There was one problem. My bride had also forgot to bring her suitcase. This delayed us about another twenty minutes, but, finally, my bride and me in my 1956 DeSoto and everyone else in my dad's 1958 Buick Special, hit the road for Columbus. We were off, my fifteen-year-old bride and me, her nineteen-year-old husband-to-be!!!

We drove up to the Columbus courthouse about a quarter 'til twelve and went in to find the judge. The courthouse closed at twelve, so this ceremony would be a short one.

We found the judge all decked out in his fishing gear, rods sittin' in the corner with his wading boots, a little brown hat on his head full of ties and jigs for fishing. He told us to stand in front of him to begin the marriage ceremony. I reached in my pocket and pulled out the ring. The judge informed me this would not be a ring ceremony, so I put the ring back in my pocket and stood staring at the judge.

He started the ceremony. I don't know what he had for breakfast, but his breath smelled terrible, a mixture of nicotine, burnt bacon, and a hint of alcohol. I don't remember much of what the judge said, but I do remember feeling hyper. When the judge said, "I now pronounce you man and wife," you could have knocked me over with a feather. I felt completely married with all the privileges. Bring on the honeymoon.

We said goodbye to our parents and decided to go to the mountains, and drove to Athens, Georgia, to spend our first night together. We checked into a motel. The price was less than ten dollars. Now, normally, the first meal should be at a place to be remembered and ours was no exception. We choose the *Pig and Whistle*. We ordered takeout and went back to the motel room, but made one stop on the way back. Well, *make that two*.

We had decided we didn't want children right off the bat, so some form of prevention had to be used. The only protection I knew of was what I called a *coin pack*, which was a rubber wrapped in an aluminum foil pack about the size of a quarter, thus a *coin pack*. You could buy them in bathrooms at gas stations or drug stores. They were always kept under the counter at the drug store and you had to ask for them.

I stopped at a large, nice drug store and went in. There were two women behind the counter. I walked around the store pretending to look, afraid to ask a woman for *you know what*. Finally, after I had walked over the store two or three times, I got up enough courage to say something to one of the women.

"Ya'll have a nice store here, Ma'am."

"Why? Thank you young man."

"Ya'll do much business here?" I said before she could say anything else.

"Why? Yes we do."

"May I help you find something?" she said, before I could come up with another question.

"I guess so Ma'am."

There was a long pause.

"What is it you are looking for?"

"Oh, I need a coin pack," I blurted out, caught by surprise. I didn't want to say *rubber*. That would have sounded too crude. I dreaded to hear what she was going to say next, but she put me at ease with her next statement.

"Why? Yes, young man. Come right over here to this counter."

What a relief. She knew exactly what I was talking about. I walked over to a long counter and began to look. The lady picked up a little box and asked me what size I needed. *Now you and I both know I had never measured it.*

"Ma'am, I'm not sure."

"Well son, we have three sizes: large, medium, and small."

Decision time!

Well, I can't go wrong by choosing a medium, I thought. Wrong!

"Well young man, we have three medium sizes: large, medium, and small."

No wonder all my friends bought theirs in the gas station bathroom. All they had to do was put in a quarter, turn the handle, and one popped out.

"I believe I'll try another medium, Ma'am."

"Good," she said, and picked up a box and handed it to me.

"This should fit your middle toe fairly well, and if it doesn't, you come back and we'll try another size."

Middle toe? What did that have to do with preventing babies? I looked at the box more closely. It read *CORN PACK FOR CALLUSES.*

"Ma'am, I don't think this size will fit either."

"Would you like to try the small size?"

"No, Ma'am."

"What about the large?"

"No, Ma'am."

"Well, we have the super-large and super-small."

"I think Ma'am I had better go home and measure it and come back later when I find out my size."

"You can measure it here son, if you like. We have a tape measure and I would be glad to help you measure it."

"Ma'am, it's beginning to feel better now. I don't think I need anything."

She followed me to the door and told me to come back when I found out my size, and if it started to give me trouble again.

Back in the car, my bride asked me how it went.

"Didn't have it," I told her. "I'll have to go to another drug store."

I was not going to go to a gas station. That was too low class.

At the next drug store, there was only one man behind the counter. When I stepped up to the counter, he asked me what I needed.

"Gimmie some rubbers."

"You need three, six, or twelve son?" he said, smiling.

"Gimmie six sir."

"Any particular brand?"
"No sir. Any brand will do."
"Dry or wet?"
"Dry sir."
"That'll be two dollars and fifty cents son."
"Here you are sir."
"Have fun son," he said with a grin as I turned to go.
"Thank you sir. I'll try."
I tried almost all night.

SATURDAY AFTERNOON AT THE MOVIES

John Dave (Pete) Fuller

Before T.V. you had to study at night if you had homework, but on Saturday afternoon there was the movies. The house was always packed—a few parents, but mostly kids. Where else could you go on a Saturday afternoon to see a double feature Western, a Batman, Superman, Green Lantern, and Buck Rodgers serial, a Tom and Jerry, and Bugs Bunny cartoon, a newsreel, the previews, and selected short subjects all for a dime? And for fifteen more cents you could buy some popcorn and a drink.

There was only one movie house in town, the Fain Theater. Mrs. Fain ran it. She sat in a little booth out front and took up the money. She had silver hair just like my grandmother and was always in a happy mood. I never remember seeing Mrs. Fain anywhere except in the little booth out in front of the movie house.

The movies played all afternoon, and if you came in the middle of a feature you just stayed 'til it played to where you came in. The best seats were as close to the front as you could get. The front row was the best, just like being in the movie.

The main features were always Westerns, starring Johnny Mack Brown, Bob Steel, Tex Ritter, Wild Bill Hickock, Hopalong Cassidy, Lash LaRue and, of course, Gene Autry and Roy Rodgers. Why else would kids pack a building on a Saturday afternoon when they could be playing? Will Bill was one of the favorites. He never drank whiskey. He drank sarsaparilla. Only the bad guys drank whiskey. Will Bill was also a peaceable man. He never lost a fight.

Bob Steel was another reason kids flocked to the movie houses on Saturday. He had nerves of steel and was a two-fisted, hard-fightin' cowboy. Hopalong Cassidy was a favorite of mine. He wore a black suit and black hat, and rode a white horse. He could fight with the best of 'em, and he never gave out of bullets.

Then there were the singing cowboys, Roy, Gene, Tex, Eddie Dean and Jimmy Wakely. They all had sidekicks, namely Frog Millhouse, Andy Devine, Fuzzy St. John and Gabby Hayes. There were so many I can't remember all of their names.

Saturday movies always had a happy ending. The cowboy got the girl and rode off into the sunset to his next adventure, only to turn once to wave to his girl. Then his horse would rear on his hind legs, and over the hill they both went to the cheering of a bunch of screaming kids.

When I grew up I wanted to be a cowboy, just like those in the movies, because they always beat the bad men and made everything right. They always stood for the good, they always got the girl, and they made the wrong right. Their guns never gave out of bullets. They never got shot, and never lost a fight, never.

I know that's not reality, but a kid can dream, can't he? I always left the movies happy and couldn't wait 'til next Saturday.

DEAD MAN'S CURVE

John Dave (Pete) Fuller

Our house was a white frame house sitting on the side of a bluff. Highway 231, a two-lane main artery to Montgomery, Alabama, was only about seventy-five feet from the front door. The traffic was heavy during the day, but slowed down at night. This was the only direct road from Montgomery to Wetumpka, Alabama, and cars and trucks traveled it twenty-four hours a day.

We lived about a mile or two from the county line in Elmore County. Now, Elmore County was a dry county, which meant no one could sell beer or whiskey there. Montgomery County was a wet county, where beer and whiskey were sold. Because of this, people would cross the county line to drink or buy their beer and whiskey at the juke joints. After they had finished their drinking, they piled in their cars and headed up 231 home to Wetumpka. Friday and Saturday night were the busiest and traffic was heavy then. This was also the time when most of the accidents happened.

One particular Saturday night was warm and humid. The air just kind of hung in limbo. If you reached out and touched it water would run down your arm. We were all sitting on our screened front porch, my daddy and mother and me, just trying to cool off, my daddy in his under shirt, mother in a cotton summer dress (most women would never wear shorts), and me in a pair of walking shorts, no shoes and no shirt.

Everything was quiet and peaceful. I was just about to fall asleep when a loud bang woke me up. It cut through the night air like a two-edged switchblade knife. Nobody had to guess what had happened. Another accident on *Dead Man's Curve*.

Mother jumped up ready to go see what had happened. She like seeing accidents. Daddy didn't want to go, but mother won out and we all crawled into our 1942 red Ford pickup and headed toward *the curve*, about a mile away.

As we pulled up and stopped, smoke was still hanging in the humid air. Daddy put me on his shoulders cause I didn't have shoes on. A big log truck was sitting half on the road and half off, smoke belching out from under the hood. The smell of gas and oil cut through the heavy air. There was another scent that I didn't recognize. It was sort of a sweet, rank smell I later learned to recognize as I grew older and had seen many more accidents. It was the smell of death.

Two black men had crawled out of the log truck, and one was holding the side of his head. Blood was trickling down his arm. The other man seemed to be okay.

On the side of the road was a car with no motor. The motor was lying in a ditch by the side of the road. A man was lying on the road by the car. He wasn't moving. His face was staring up at me, but his body was lying face down. The other man was still in the car hunched over the steering wheel. He wasn't moving either. That sweet rank smell was stronger close to the car. My mother threw up and had to go back to the truck. Both men were dead.

Soon other people began arriving at the scene and the silence was broken by a lot of talking and shouting. It seems the two men in the car couldn't handle *Dead Man's Curve*. They had hit the log truck head on. They must have been going 100 miles per hour when they hit. That's where the speedometer needle had stuck. They were coming from the county line direction. There was an empty whiskey bottle on the front seat of the car.

I'm older now as I write this story. I've seen many more accidents, but that one still clouds my memory. Two men died on that muggy Saturday night.

Wives and children were left with no husband or father, victims of that lone whiskey bottle and *Dead Man's Curve*.

Song: Dead Man's Curve

THE HOSPITAL WARD

John Dave (Pete) Fuller

In the forties and fifties, going in the hospital was an experience you were not likely to forget for a long time. Doctors and nurses did scrub before operations, and after examining each patient. All the equipment was sterilized after each use. There was no throw-away equipment; even the needles were used over and over again. AIDS was something you sent to a foreign country after an earthquake, or some other natural disaster. Compared to hospitals today some things were pretty primitive. There were not many private rooms and the ones that were available were very small, with a sink, and a commode, a bed, and one chair. Private rooms were for the well-to-do. Most common folk were put in a ward.

The wards were long, dormitory-type rooms that could accommodate many patients at a time, up to ten, and maybe as many as twenty. The only thing that separated patients was a thin cloth on a metal pipe, like a shower curtain, that could be closed by the doctors and nurses when they were doctoring you.

The patients in the wards had many different ailments, and in the mid-fifties, having a bruised and bleeding spleen (as diagnosed by the orderly), I was confined to a ward. They put me in for observation I suppose, because they didn't give me any medication, and I never did see a doctor. There was only one nurse for the entire ward. There were male and female wards, but most of the nurses were female, and if something had to be done that required a man, then the orderly took care of it. He was a big black man who always smoked a cigar. I wondered why he smoked a cigar, but later figured it out. If I had had one I would have smoked it too. I'll get to that part later.

Some of the patients were very colorful and from all walks of life. I remember one man who had a neck problem and was lying flat of his back with weights attached to lines that were hooked to a face strap under his chin and around his head. He could not move unless a nurse came and unhooked the weights. He sometimes had to yell to get the nurse because there were no call buttons. Sometimes the nurse was late and they had to change his bed linen.

One man had a broken leg, but they could not put it in a cast 'til the swelling went down. The broken leg was about twice the size of the other leg.

There were various other ailments. Some had stomach problems and were constantly throwing up, while there were others with opposite end problems.

The smell of the ward changed hourly, and every smell was different. I liked the cigar smell over all the others and would have smoked one if the orderly had given me one.

One day the man with the neck problems tried to get out of his rig and almost broke his neck, because he had to go to the bathroom and no one would come. The poor guy with the broken leg never bothered to call, the smell usually brought the nurse. I was lucky. I could walk, and when things got bad I usually found an outside door or an open window for some fresh air.

I never ate the food. You shouldn't have to ask why.

They let me go home after four days. I was the first to leave and gladly gave up my bed. The other nine were still there. They never really found out what was wrong with me, but the orderly said I had a bruised spleen, so I took his word for it.

MY FIRST FOOTBALL LETTER

John Dave (Pete) Fuller

Well, I finally made it to the tenth grade and my first year on the football team. I guess every boy who grew up in the fifties wanted to play football. Well, most of them did.

Football was a gladiator sport where the strongest win and the winner is the hero. Naturally every boy wants to be the hero. I quickly found out that the road to being a hero was long and tough. There were long afternoon practices which sometimes lasted 'til dark.

Since I was a tenth grader I had the privilege of being on the "B" team. U This meant that every week we had to learn the opposing team's plays so we could scrimmage against the "A" team or varsity. Since I played halfback I usually played the role of the opposing team's star half-back. This was not an envious spot to be in, as I quickly learned. I usually got the $#! & knocked out of me on every play, but I learned how to defend myself or get killed. The varsity players showed no mercy, so neither did I after the first week. I first became better known the day I ran into our varsity first string end and broke his arm. All varsity players were advised to drink more milk after that incident. Now I was a marked man, and every varsity player was after me, but I didn't care. I actually enjoyed the physical contact. I guess you could call it a natural high.

As each week passed our "B" team got tougher and meaner, giving the varsity more competition. They knew what to expect from the opposing team because our "B" team challenged them every practice day.

Our varsity compiled a good record that year. They won nine and lost one, and were heroes every one. I did get to play one complete varsity game, which we won, and at the end of the season I had earned my first football letter and the respect of all the varsity players. Someone asked me if it was worth all the black eyes, sore muscles, hard hits, and knock out punches I received. My answer was yes. I became a survivor because of that year. Why I even learned to like the smell of the Atomic Bomb

they used for sore muscles, and the smelling sauce they used to revive you after you were knocked out.
Song: Football Hero

THE GOOD OLE DAYS
John Dave (Pete) Fuller

They say the 1950s were the *good ole days*. From 1950 to 1959 I grew from an eleven-year-old fifth grader to a twenty-year-old married man with a newborn child, born February 24, 1959.

School was different in 1950. Most of the teachers were women; the principal was a man. My first male teacher was the band teacher in the seventh grade. There were two other male teachers, one in the ninth and one in the twelfth. They oiled the wood floors, and recess meant playing ball, swinging marbles, jacks, tops, dodgeball, or most any game, madeup or real.

Every student looked up to their teacher and respected their authority. If we misbehaved we were paddled. We never questioned the teacher's judgment and our parents always took the teacher's side. There were some exceptions, but not many.

The big bang theory was taught, but everybody believed God created the world. I don't know when God was put in the pledge, but nobody complained when He was. The Lord's Prayer was prayed at the beginning of every school day. Nobody ever complained about it. If you didn't want to participate you just didn't say the prayer and that was that.

Nothing was ever said about a dress code, because everybody dressed in a proper way. Girls usually wore dresses and never showed their navel. Skirt lengths were below the knees. I never saw a girl trying to pull a skirt down because it kept crawling up between the knees and you know where. Some things are best left to the imagination only, to be revealed when you are able to handle responsibility, like marriage.

Petticoats were in style. Some girls wore a bunch. I remember dating some who had trouble getting in the front seat of the car, and when they did get in she couldn't see out the window. I was glad when that trend died.

Boys' clothes were different. When I really dressed up I wore a white sport coat, a pink shirt, black-pegged pants, and white buck shoes. Belts were very narrow and so were ties. I actually wore creased blue jeans to school that were not faded. Faded jeans were for work only. When I wore a short sleeve shirt the sleeves were turned up one cuff. Some of my shirts in elementary school were made of flour sacks. In the late fifties nylon seethru shirts were popular. Of course a tee shirt was worn under the shirt.

All cars were recognizable. Fords were Fords, Chevrolets looked like Chevy's, Buicks looked like a Buick. You could just about name any car driving down the road.

I always rode a yellow school bus to school 'til I reached the tenth grade. U Then my father let me use our Forty Eight Buick to drive to school. Sometimes I would ride with a friend who built hot rods. In the spring we would ride in his stripped-down rod, which consisted of a frame, a windshield, a motor, a front seat, a steering wheel, and no body. There was a place to put a rumble seat, just in case girls wanted to ride. This car was wide open. I guess you could call it a poor man's convertible.

A car with only one headlight at night was called a *popeye*. When you were dating and driving down the road, if you yelled "Popeye!" before your date you got to kiss her one time. If she beat you she could slap you or let you kiss her. There was not a lot of slapping that went on. I usually saved up my kisses 'til we parked, and by that time it didn't matter anyway.

Usually after a date a coke and burger were in order, and there were plenty of places to eat. There was Cordell's Sugar and Spice, The Parkmore, and The Cottage. You usually went to the most popular one at the time. Nobody went in. You stayed in the car and were served by a carhop. The carhops were girls. I don't ever remember seeing a boy carhop.

One Friday night one of my classmates challenged me to a drag race. Drag racing was popular in the 50s. He owned a '50 Chevy, or at least his dad did, and he said his Chevy would run circles around my '48 Buick. I agreed to race, but not for only a quarter mile. My old Buick was heavier than the Chevy and would not build up much speed in a quarter mile, so we agreed on a mile and a half. I knew it would take me at least a half mile to build up speed, and once the ole Buick got rolling it would move on.

Well, we started and I pushed the petal to the floor. He shot ahead of me, and at the quarter mile he was two car lengths ahead. At the half mile he was only a car length ahead. I was steadily gaining ground. When we reached the mile marker I was dead even and I could tell he was beginning to panic. I held her steady and the speedometer was touching 100 and climbing. The last half mile I lost sight of the Chevy. I was clocking 115 and the old Buick had settled down to cruise speed. You'd never known we were doing 115 if the speedometer hadn't shown it. The moral of this story is never race a jackass with a racehorse.

Well, the *good ole days* have come and gone. Nothing left but memories. Those days are lost forever, a fog that disappeared with the rising sun. But you know, sometimes on a cool fall day, when it's cloudy and maybe a light misty rain is falling, and I'm drivin' down a long lonely stretch of road, I feel like I'm back in the 50s and sittin' behind the wheel of my old '48 Buick. I pass all the eating places with the carhops. My buddy passes me in his stripped-down rod with four girls in the rumble seat (Hey, one of those girls was my girl!). I pass my old high school. The big ole oak tree in the front is still there, and Mr. B. is standing on the front steps looking for skippers. I turn the corner and suddenly it's Friday night. The football field is lit up and you can hear the band playing, the cheerleaders cheering, the crowd roaring, and suddenly, it's 2004 and I'm back in the real world driving my 2003 Buick Century. The next cool day I'm going to look for that lonely stretch of road and go back to the *good ole days*.

Alternate last paragraphs.

Well, the *good ole days* have come and gone. Nothing left but the memories. Those days are lost forever, a fog that disappeared with the rising sun. But you know on a cool fall day, when it's cloudy and maybe a light misty rain is fallin', and I'm drivin' down a long lonely stretch of road, I feel like I'm back in the 50s and sittin' behind the wheel of my '48 Buick. I pass all the eating places with the carhops, my buddy passes me in his stripped-down rod with four girls in the rumble seat—Hey, one of those girls was my girl! My old high school with the big ole oak tree in the front is still there, and Mr. B., our principal, is standing on the front steps looking for class skippers. I turn the corner and suddenly it's Friday night, the football field is lit up, you can hear the band playing, the cheerleaders cheering, the crowd roaring, and, suddenly, it's 2004 and I'm back in the real world of the 21 St century driving my 2003 Buick Century.

Now and then, on one of those cool fall days when a light misty rain is fallin', I jump in my Buick and start to drive, looking for that lonely stretch of road. Who knows, I might find it and never come back.

Song: Those Were the Days

WHERE'S THE BATHROOM?

John Dave (Pete) Fuller

When I was about six years old we moved to the country. Our first house had indoor plumbing, which was much like city plumbing except there was no sewer. The toilet had a direct line to a huge gulley about fifty feet on the backside of our yard. The gulley was about seventy-five feet deep, and all of the waste from our house—kitchen and bathroom—dumped into the gulley. About once a month my daddy would dump a sack of lime into the gulley to take care of the smell, and any germs that might exist. This worked well for several years.

When I would invite friends over to play, one of our favorite games was to flush the toilet, run out the back door and scramble to the edge of the gulley before the waste dumped out of the waste pipe and fell seventyfive feet to the bottom of the gulley. This consumed hours of playtime, many gallons of water, and several rolls of toilet paper unless some adult caught us.

We lived in this house 'til I was about seven, then moved to another house about two miles down the road. This house was smaller and didn't have a gulley. I knew right off I was not going to like this house with no gulley.

We moved in the dead of winter and our first night at the new house the mercury dipped down to around twenty degrees. This house was heated with a potbellied wood stove, and I didn't have much to do but sit by the stove and try to stay warm 'til bedtime.

About nine o'clock, thirty minutes before bedtime, the urge hit me. You all know what I'm talking about. Well, I jumped up and asked daddy where the bathroom was. I hadn't bothered to locate that room cause I had been looking for gulleys all day.

"Come on son," my daddy said, and he took me out to the back porch. I thought this was strange since it was cold out there. In our last house the bathroom was closer to the bedrooms. My daddy pointed out into the dark with his flashlight to a small-looking shed.

"There it is son," he said.

"There what is?" I asked.

"The bathroom son," daddy answered. "See that little house out there in the dark about fifty yards down the back path."

I'd noticed the little house earlier, but thought it was the smokehouse, you know, where all the meat is cured. I was about to discover that the difference between the smokehouse and the outhouse is that the outhouse has a half moon cut in the door.

Well, since it was twenty degrees outside, you know I didn't tarry at the outhouse very long. The only problem I had was finding the right size hole, cause there were three holes: Papa Bear, Mama Bear, and Baby Bear. I choose the Baby Bear one cause I would have fell through the others.

It was about six months before we installed an indoor bathroom, and 'til that time I usually made my trips to the outhouse in the daytime when it was warmer. I really missed that gully though.

O.M. BRATTON (Mr. B.)
John Dave (Pete) Fuller

Small in stature, maybe 5'6" or 5'7". Dark hair combed straight back. Slightly heavy eyebrows. A very gentle nature. Might have weighed 140 lbs. on a rainy day. He normally wore a white shirt and tie, and dark trousers. He was always neat and clean shaven. To see him in a crowd you would never give a second glance. Just an average everyday man traveling through this corridor called life.

Mr. B. was the principal of the Wetumpka High School, and when I entered the seventh grade I became part of the high school. I found out pretty quick that Mr. B. ran a tight ship. He was nice, but didn't put up with any foolishness. As a seventh grader I found out early who was the boss. Mr. B was.

Mr. B. allowed a lot of flexibility in school. We were allowed a thirty minute recess and could go to Fred Sides grocery store off campus if we wanted to, but better not be late for class. Lunch was very relaxed. The 7th, 8th, and 9th ate first, then the 10th, 11th, and 1 2th. You could sit anywhere you wanted. We stood in line and paid for our lunch as we went in the door. Mrs. B., Mr. B's wife, took up the money.

Mr. B. had a nose for spotting trouble and always seemed to know before trouble started where it was going to start. One afternoon on the school bus two boys began to argue and everybody knew a fight was about to start, we thought. In popped Mr. B. He marched down the bus aisle, grabbed each kid by the nape of the neck and drug them off the bus, taking them to his office. There were ten buses lined up to leave school. How Mr. B. knew which bus I'll never know, but he did.

After football practice some of us football players would slip into the school building to drink some cold water out of the hail water fountain. We knew how to jimmy the lock on the hail door leading into the school. Not only could we quench our thirst, but it was fun sliding down the greased hail floor on our cleats on the bottom of our shoes. This went on for several weeks.

One day after practice I was the only one thirsty, so I slipped around the gym corner, quickly jimmied the lock, took off down the hall and started sliding on my cleats. What fun. I slid right up to the water fountain. Mr. B. was holding the pedal down for me to get a cool drink of water. He had a wide grin on his face. I don't know where he came from, but there he was, grin and all. He didn't put me in jail or paddle me. I just had to help oil the floors and pick up trash for about a month during my free time. Mr. B. did make sure the gym water fountain would produce cold water, and we were told we could go to the ice house for cool refreshment after practice.

Mr. B. was the friend of the student and we all knew it. Some hardheads would not admit it, but deep down knew it was true. To prove this point, Mr. B. did not allow smokin' or chewin' in school and counseled kids not to smoke. He did however realize some kids would slip around and smoke anyway, and if a child brought a note from home signed by the parent stating that their child could smoke, then they were allowed to smoke in the smoking area out behind the canning plant, but only at recess.

No gambling was allowed anywhere, anytime. If you were caught gambling the punishment was swift and to the point. Students had a choice: either three days suspension or corporal punishment (one to an unlimited number of licks applied to your backside). Mr. B did not paddle girls. The female P.E. teacher did that if it was required. Girls did receive three day passes if necessary. I don't ever remember any girl being sent home during my high school days.

One day during my senior year I was taking a makeup test in Mr. B's office when three sophomores were brought in for shooting dice out behind the gym. I stopped working on my test and got up to leave, though I had not finished taking my test. Mr. B motioned for me to stay seated. The boys were lined in front of Mr. B's desk. Everything got very quiet. The tension began to mount, especially when Mr. B. pulled out a thick leather strap about two feet long, three fourths of an inch thick, with a leather handle. There were several holes drilled through the flat part, the business end of the strap. Nobody said a word. One student was visibly nervous, one had a smirk on his face, the other showed no emotion. Mr. B. broke the silence.

"What do you boys have to say for yourself?"

Silence. Finally, one boy spoke.

"I'm sorry Mr. B. I won't ever do it again. I thought it was just a game."

Silence again. A second boy said the boy with the smirk made him do it (a likely story I thought). The kid with the smirk never said a word; just stood and smirked.

"Well boys," said Mr. B., "you all have two choices. You can go home for three days, or take three licks from the strap."

The nervous boy decided to take three days. Mr. B. asked him to move over by the door. The other two said they would take three licks from the strap. The kid with the smirk said he would take his licks first. He was taller than Mr. B. and weighed more. He acted as though he could take anything from Mr. B.

Mr. B took a chair and put it in front of his desk and told the smirkin' kid to lean over the back of the chair and place his hands in the seat. This pretty much bared his butt and leveled the playing field. His jeans were stretched very tight. Mr. B had him remove his billfold and place it on the desk. The kid did so with a smile, and leaned over the chair again, and kind of wiggled both legs as if to say, "If you think you are man enough, go ahead and let me have all you got."

Mr. B. did. The first lick lifted the boy's feet and butt about an inch or two straight up. The smirk left and a grimace appeared. Tears began to well up in his eyes. This hurt my butt and I didn't take the lick. The kid didn't wiggle his legs this time. They hung kind of limp. The second lick brought more tears, more hurt. I thought his butt was going to catch fire. The third lick brought a scream; tears were streaming down his face. Mr. B. told him to go in the restroom in his office, wash his face and compose himself. He just about jumped through the door. Mr. B. told him there was clean underwear on the shelf in case he needed some.

Mr. B. turned to the other kid, who was visibly shaking.

"Mr. B. can I still choose the three days?"

Mr. B. said yes, and smiled as the kid quickly left to sign out for home. I buried myself in my makeup test, hoping Mr. B. would not look at me. He didn't.

Later everyone asked me what happened in there. I told them a few licks were passed and a few vacation days given out for shootin' craps behind the gym.

"You mean Mr. B. actually paddled somebody?"

"Yep."

"What was it like?"

"I'll put it to you this way. My butt is still aching and I didn't get paddled."

The big kid lost his smirk and turned out to be a well-behaved student. The other two students came back to school after their three day vacation.

All was well on the school front.

THE SOAPBOX DERBY AND MR. SPUDNUTT

John Dave (Pete) Fuller

In the early fifties the Soapbox Derby was an annual event in the good ole US of A. Every major city had trial races for ten to twelve-year-olds and the winner in each city got to go to Akron, Ohio, for the finals. The winner there was the Soapbox Derby champion, an honor any ten or twelve-yearold would cherish.

A friend of mine, Wayne Smith, was going to enter the race in Montgomery, Alabama, and he convinced me to enter. In order to enter you had to have a sponsor. My father owned a public swimming pool called Willow Springs and he sponsored me. My father asked Mr. Ryals, a carpenter, to help me build a racecar. He did most of the work. I just kind of looked on. It was a wood car with a canvas cover. The wheels were standard ball-bearing and were all furnished by the ones in charge of the race. Course you had to buy the wheels from them.

I felt a little guilty about not really building my car, but on race day there were cars with sheet metal covering and professional upholstering. No ten or twelve-year-old could have possibly built those cars. Actually, I think my friend had the only car in the race that was built by the driver. None of the others were homemade. I guess my car was half and half. I sort of felt sorry for my friend, because he was the only one who actually built his car. Needless to say, his car and mine were not the sleekest-looking cars in the race. On a scale of 1 to 10 his was a one and mine a two. Our wheels looked good though, just like everybody else's.

After my car was built I had to practice driving the thing down a hill. There were several hills over in Redland, named because of the red clay soil that were perfect for practice, long hills and hardly any traffic. The hill we choose was steep and long, and my car reached a speed close to 30 miles per hour. After several trips down I got the hang of it. I felt like a genuine race car driver. Billy Joe Ryals was in charge of the pit crew. He got to ride the car too.

Race day finally arrived and we loaded my car on the back of our pickup truck, a green International. Everybody gathered at Capitol Chevrolet, the race sponsor, and every driver registered, and our cars were inspected for hidden motors, illegal wheel grease, extra weights, and anything that might give a driver an unfair advantage. There was also a competition for the best-looking car. My friend and I finished dead last. In fact I don't think the judges even looked at our cars except maybe from a distance. Our cars were homemade for racing, not looks.

The race was held on Dexter Avenue. Two cars raced at a time, off a wooden ramp about a foot high, sloped on one end. This gave each car a faster and equal start. My friend lost his first race and was eliminated. I won my first race and we had to load my car on our pickup at the bottom of Dexter Avenue, and travel back around to the starting point.

On the way back around my daddy told me that one racer, who had already won two races, had a plan that gave him an advantage. Dexter Avenue was built so the water would run off from the center to the sides. It was slightly more curved downhill to the right and left of the center line. He told me when I left the ramp to steer to the right slightly, then back to the center. By doing this you would pick up speed faster and be ahead of the other car when you arrived back on the center line. Well, the shortest distance between two points is a straight line. The other car got to point B before I did and when I reached the center of the street I was half a car length behind and could never catch up. I lost the race by half a car length.

There was much speculation afterwards as to what went wrong, and why I lost the race. Everybody had a theory. My theory was I finished half a car length behind the other car. That was the reason I lost the race. The car that gets from point A to B the fastest wins the race. The other car got there before I did. Mr. Spudnutt sponsored the other car, Imagine gettin' beat by a Spudnutt.

Meanwhile, remember the other driver who had already won two races. Well, he was in the final race. Both cars were lined up on the starting ramp, a black sleek-looking car, and a red, white, and blue one. The red, white, and blue car veered to the right and then back to the left. He was a full car length ahead of the sleek black car. It looked like the race was over from the start. The red, white, and blue car held his lead for three-quarters of the race, then the sleek black car zipped by the red, white, and blue car like he was standin' still. Nobody could believe their eyes. The black car had won.

The driver of the black car had two brothers who had won the Derby the two previous years. The talk was that winning races must run in the family. Anyway, the winner was declared and it was all over but the shoutin'. So we thought!

We loaded up my car on the truck and headed back to Capitol Chevrolet to look for my daddy. He was nowhere around. When we drove up and parked there was a large crowd gathered out front. I asked someone what was going on, and they told me that someone had protested the race. I asked them who would do such a thing. They said some guy had removed the winner's wheels and found an illegal lubricant on the ball bearings, namely graphite. Well, the wheels were sealed, but a small hole had been drilled in each wheel and graphite had been squirted in. I asked who had found this out and they said some man in a white Stetson hat, a white shirt, and blue khaki pants. I climbed up on a car to look over the crowd to get a better look. Sure enough there he was in the middle of the crowd, black race car jacked up, all the wheels off, the man in the white Stetson, sleeves rolled up, graphite on both hands showing everybody. I found my daddy, white hat and all.

The officials of the race still declared the black car the winner. They said it wasn't graphite in the wheels. Well, every kid from first grade on that's ever chewed on a pencil and got pencil lead all over their hands can identify graphite, and graphite was not supposed to be in the sealed wheels, not to mention the small holes drilled in each wheel, which was also against the rules.

That was the end of the Soapbox Derby in Montgomery, Alabama. To win by breaking the rules is not right in anybody's book, whether it be racing, baseball, football, or anything. Winning is not winning if you create an unfair advantage. Yes, I tried to take advantage of a sloping street and lost my race. The red, white, and blue car did the same thing and won every race except the last race. Everyone at the race could see what he was doing, including the judges. It was not against the rules. All the drivers could have done the same thing. Graphite was against the rules and everyone knew it.

My daddy was an honest man. I never knew him to beat anybody out of anything. He told me after the race, "Son, you got beat fair and square. There's always another time and another race. Life is like that."

It took me a while to get over getting beat by Mr. Spudnutt though, but I did.

BEGINNER BAND 1951

John Dave (Pete) Fuller

In the seventh grade I decided to learn how to play the trumpet. Since I didn't have a trumpet one had to be found. I told my parents and my daddy set out to purchase one, and finally brought one home. It was in a small black case that was lined with purple cloth. The instrument was gold-looking, and was engraved all over the bell. There were three valves with pearl buttons, and a mouthpiece to fit in the end of the tubing at one end of the horn. I was thrilled to get this instrument and couldn't wait to start beginner band.

Mr. Welch was the band teacher. He had a lot of blonde hair and smoked a pipe. He played the saxophone and the flute, which he demonstrated for us in band class. Some of the students told me he had also been a boxer when he was in the Army, and played in the Army band.

Our band class was held in the high school auditorium. On the first day, there were flutes, saxophones, trombones, clarinets, drums, and trumpets. We all were sitting down when Mr. Welch came in, except one kid who was a clown. Mr. Welch took the kid to a seat and set him down. He told us all that there would be no clowns in band and that we should come into band class and sit down and take out instruments and get ready to play. We could talk, but when he came into the room we should stop talking and listen to what he had to say.

We were all placed in sections according to our instruments: flutes together, clarinets together, and so forth. All the trumpets took out our instruments. It was at this point I noticed my trumpet looked different from the others. My trumpet was shorter and looked smaller. I didn't say anything. I was a little embarrassed but my trumpet looked good with all the engraving on the bell. Mr. Welch came over and took my trumpet and looked at it. I thought, I'm in trouble now. He's singled me out from all the other trumpets. After a long silence and a few mmmhhhhhhs and mmmhhhhhhs, he told me that I didn't have a trumpet, but I had a coronet. Oh no, I thought. My daddy blew a hundred dollars on a coronet and not a trumpet. Mr. Welch told me that I could play a coronet and that it sounded like a trumpet, but the tone was mellower than a trumpet, and that coronets usually played the melody because of their mellow sound. He said the coronet had a conical bore, and that trumpets had a cylindrical bore, and they were the same length. Mine just had more turns in the tubing.

Well, it was time to start playing those instruments, but we first had to learn how to put them together properly. The clarinets came in five pieces and had a little wooden reed that fit on the end of the thing. The flutes were in three pieces but had no reed attached to them. The saxophones had three pieces with a reed, and the trombones were two pieces and a mouthpiece. The trumpets and my coronet only had a mouthpiece that fit in the end of the small tubing.

It took a while for the clarinets, flutes, and saxophones to learn, but they finally did learn to make a sound. Now we could learn to make a sound with the horn. It took a while, because Mr. Welch had to show each one of us individually.

Finally, we were all at least making a sound, some better than others. It was time to start playing music. We turned to a page in our instruction book that had a bunch of lines and little round-looking things called notes. You had to look at a note and decide which note it was and mash down one of the pearl buttons according to the name of the note. There were Gs, Es, As, and Bs, and a bunch more, but to begin with we just worked on a few.

On about the third day it was time for all of us to play out notes together. Mr. Welch counted off 1-2-3-4 and we all played. It sounded like a B-29 bomber with engine trouble about to crash. We got better as the weeks went by and after much practice we were playing songs. At first the songs were simple—Row, Row, Row Your Boat; Mary's Little Lamb; Music In The Air—and we all played the melody, but by the end of the year we were playing harmony and the melody. We also learned some scales and how to tune our instrument and play in tune with everyone else. Mr. Welch told us if we worked very hard we could move up to the Jr. Band next year. We all looked forward to that. We also learned Mr. Welch was pretty nice as long as we practiced and worked hard. Beginner band was fun.

Song: *76 Trombones* or *Strike Up The Band*
Alternate Ending.

On about the third day we began to try to play our notes together. Mr. Welch would count off 1-2-3-4 and we all played. It sounded like a B-29 bomber with engine trouble about to crash. We got better as the weeks went by and after much practice we were playing songs. At first the songs were simple: Row, Row, Row Your Boat; Mary Had A Little Lamb; Music In The Air, and London Bridge. At first we all played the melody, but soon began to play in harmony. Mr. Welch would walk around and punch you in the belly with a baton to see if you were supporting the sound. We all learned to watch out for him and would tighten up when we saw him coming.

That year we learned to play some scales and how to play in tune with everyone else. We also learned discipline—even the clown—and how to work together as a group. Mr. Welch told us that if we worked hard we could move up to the Jr. Band the next year. We all looked forward to that. Mr. Welch was a nice teacher as long as we practiced and worked hard, but could scare you to death if you didn't practice. Beginner band was fun. I can still smell Mr. Welch's pipe.

Song: The Band Played On (Casey Would Waltz With the Strawberry Blonde)

SCHOOL CLOTHES 1945

John Dave (Pete) Fuller

Every year before school started my mother would take me to town to buy my school clothes. I always looked forward to this, because we usually stayed most of the day in the big city of Montgomery. We usually went on a Saturday when everybody went to town. Montgomery was huge compared to Wetumpka. Course we lived in the country and going to any town on Saturday was a treat.

We usually left fairly early and got there about the time the stores were opening. I guess everybody else must have left about the same time 'cause they got there about the same time we did. What a sight.

Dexter Avenue was the main street with all of the stores lined up one side and down the other. There was Silvers, Kress, Newberrys, Montgomery Fair, Sears and Roebuck, Kris' Hotdog Stand, Webbers, and Liggett's Drug Store at the end of Dexter across from Court Square. You could drive down Dexter and go around the fountain and back up Dexter. You could park on either side of Dexter.

Mother would usually take me and buy all my clothes first thing. We would buy blue jeans, shirts, socks, shorts, and tennis shoes, and maybe a pair of Sunday shoes. One time I got a green sport jacket you could zip up in the front and the sleeves had elastic bands around the wrists. I wore that jacket to death. It was my favorite.

With shopping out of the way fun time began. I usually hit all the toy departments first, then a bananna split at Liggett's Drug Store. By then I usually found mother and we had lunch at the lunch counter at Newberrys, but sometime ate at Silvers or Kress. I liked Newberrys best and usually U ordered turkey and dressing with cranberry sauce.

After lunch mother shopped some more and I took in the larger toy department at Sears and Roebuck. They had everything a kid would ever want there—trains, trucks, bicycles, toy guns, tents, wagons, scooters, cowboy outfits, baseball gloves—and of course all the stuff girls liked, which I wouldn't be caught dead looking at that stuff.

Soon it was time to go home so I found my mother and we packed everything in our car and headed for home. I had all my school clothes for another year and my green coat. I was fixed up. I couldn't wait 'til next year Course Christmas wasn't too far off, but that's another story.

Song: Down Town

SATURDAY NIGHT BASEBALL

John Dave (Pete) Fuller

It was the bottom of the 5th and the Cubs were leading the Phillies 3 to 2. All the sounds were there: the crack of the bat, the roar of the crowd, the thud of the catcher's mitt, *hum-babe, strrrr-ike-yur-out*, and everything that made baseball sound like baseball.

I never went to a big league game, but as I lay there every Saturday night, sometimes I could smell the hide of a new ball, the saddle soap and leather of a well-used glove, or the aroma of a good chew of plug tobacco. And yes, even the crowd had a smell of its own, a mixture of Pabst, Falstaff, and Miller all rolled into one. It was hard to believe all that could travel over the radio waves. A child's imagination can work wonders though.

Saturday night was always a special night. The ritual was always the same, never varying. Supper, then baths (everybody bathed on Saturday night), followed by a talcum rub, and then off to bed. Those hot, balmy summer nights always seemed cooler on Saturday. What a delight Saturday night was, not a care to worry you after a good supper and a good bath, and lying there in bed with your daddy listening to Saturday night baseball.

Daddy usually slept with an undershirt and boxer shorts and I slept with P.J.'s on. They always smelled like sunshine on a warm spring day. The sunshine smell, talcum powder, and all the sounds of baseball mingled with the heated radio tubes on a balmy night will always be Saturday night to me. No other night smells or sounds the same.

The Cubs finally won the game in the bottom of the ninth on a Texas leaguer single. Game over and radio off. Time to go to sleep.

"Goodnight daddy."
"Goodnight son."
"Who plays next Saturday?"
"Go to sleep son."

Ah, the smells and sounds of Saturday night baseball.
Song: Take me out to the Ballgame

GRAMMAR SCHOOL
John Dave (Pete) Fuller

1945 was a banner year for me. I was excited because it was my first time to go to school. My mother took me to town and bought me brand new clothes. I also got to eat at Newberrys, and look at all the toys, a real treat. Besides Newberrys, there was Kress (I called it Kressies), Silvers, Montgomery Fair, Sears and Roebuck, and Webbers. What a sight for a six-year-old, the sounds, the smell, all those people, and cars everywhere. What a world!

On the first day of school my mother took me. I'll never forget that day. Where did all these kids come from? The school was red brick with a big circular drive in front and a sidewalk straight up to the front door. There was a big flagpole right in the middle of the school yard. We all met in a big auditorium right in the middle of the school. We sang the Star Spangled Banner, gave the pledge of allegiance to the flag (everybody put their hand over their heart), and a preacher got up and said a few words and prayed. We found out which room to go to. There were three first grade teachers: Mrs. Melton, Mrs. Daniel, and Mrs. Kelley. I was assigned to Mrs. Kelley's room.

There were about twenty of us in Mrs. Kelley's class, about ten boys and ten girls. It was the first time I'd ever seen that many girls in one place. The room was very colorful, with pictures and other things on the wall, which I later learned were the alphabet and numbers. There was a cardboard playhouse in one corner and tables with chairs to sit on. When we went to the auditorium we took our chairs and marched single file.

The first day of school ended at noon, but every day after we stayed all day. After lunch every day we had to take a thirty minute nap on our pallets, and then on some days we would go to Mrs. Melton's room and listen to her tell us stories. Sometimes on sunny days we would take our pallets outside for our nap. One day I and a friend got hot in the sun, so we crawled under the school house and went to sleep. Our class went to Mrs. Melton's room without us. When we woke up we went back to our room and found no one there, so we just played with all the toys. After about an hour nobody had come back to our room, so we wandered out in the hall looking for our class and found out everybody was looking for us. Everybody thought we had been kidnapped or something.

I learned a lot in the first grade: how to read, how to draw, and how to play a bunch of games. I even had a girlfriend. Her name was June and she had a twin sister whose name was Joan. It took me a while to figure out who was who.

About twice a week all three first grades would gather in the auditorium and sing. Mrs. Kelley would play the piano and Mrs. Daniels would teach us songs. I don't know where Mrs. Melton was. Maybe she was somewhere making up stories. I enjoyed singing and later in the third grade I took voice lessons from Mrs. Bateman, who was blind. My first solo was Three Little Trees. I also learned to play the tonette in Mrs. Venable's class and learned how to kiss girls in the cloak room. The cloak room was also where the teacher took you to paddle you if you were bad. I liked the kissing better.

There was this kid named Elijah, who was the class bully. Everybody was scared of him, and when Elijah would bully you he would squint his eyes together and make himself look mean. One day we were playing ball on the backside of the playground and Elijah started to bully me. He squinted his eyes and looked mean. I balled up my fist and hit him right between those squinted-up eyes. We were good friends after that, and he didn't bully me anymore.

My second grade teacher was Mrs. Keeble. I don't remember much about the second grade, except I threw up one day and smelled like vomit all day. Boy was I glad to get home that day.

Mrs. Greer was my fourth grade teacher. She also taught the fifth grade along with us. It was fun being with older kids. We learned more than the three R's that year.

The fourth grade was the first time I got sent to the principal for fighting, fighting with a fifth grader. I don't remember his name except that he was a lot taller than me, and he kept hitting me on top of my head. I could only hit him in the stomach. Mr. Waldrip, the principal, told us we could put on the boxing gloves or take a paddling. I told him I'd just as soon take a paddling. I was tired of getting hit on the top of the head. Mr. Waldrip didn't paddle us on the head.

In the fifth grade I took band under Mr. Welch. I tried the trombone but didn't learn to play it. I later learned to play the trumpet. Mrs. Cousins was my teacher, and that year they moved us three times, from an old white frame building next to a railroad track, to a room behind the auditorium stage, and, finally, to a regular classroom. It was this year that I learned how the earth was created. They said there was a big explosion on the sun and all of a sudden the planets appeared around the sun. I never did believe that, but I always put that on the tests and made a good grade.

Mrs. Cousins had a big picture of an owl hanging above the front blackboard. The owl had big eyes and no matter what part of the room you were in the owl was always looking at you. Mrs. Cousins told us the owl was watching to see if we counted on our fingers when we added or subtracted. I solved that problem real quick. I put my hands behind my back so the owl could not see my hands. Besides, I knew that the owl was a night creature and couldn't see well in the daylight.

In the sixth grade I learned to draw. Mrs. Cobb was my teacher and she spent a lot of time teaching me how to draw. I still like to draw to this day. Girls began to play a bigger role in my life at this point. I had several girlfriends that year.

Six years passed pretty quickly and through it all I learned a lot. I don't think I'll ever forget grammar school and that certain smell it had caused by a certain blend of all the books, crayons, oiled wooden floors, coal furnaces, pencil shavings, and kids of all shapes and sizes. The teachers will also remain in my memory forever: Mrs. Kelley, Mrs. Daniel, Mrs. Melton, Mrs. Keeble, Mrs. Venable, Mrs. Greer, Mrs. Cousins, Mrs. Young, Mr. Welch, and Mrs. Cobb. They helped to shape a life that probably wouldn't have made it had it not been for them.

Goodbye Hohenburg Memorial, my old grammar school. They razed you and buried you I know not where, but you'll always be there etched in my memory forever. Goodbye my friend.

Song: School Days

BORN ON THE WRONG SIDE OF THE BLANKET

John Dave (Pete) Fuller

I was born in 1939. They said that I was an illegitimate child. I guess that meant I was not legitimate. I later found out that I was also a bastard, born on the wrong side of the blanket, but that didn't bother me none since I didn't know what any of those words meant anyway. I grew up in the Heart of Dixie, in central Alabam'. Growing up was fun, especially in the big city of Montgomery, Alabama.

My adopted mother (I was adopted when I was three days old) wanted to throw me out our second story window when I was about two weeks old. My adopted daddy talked her out of it and put me in bed with him. I slept with him 'til I was durn near five-years-old. My grandad, Dad Hicks, and my grandma, Grade Hicks, took care of me during the day cause both my parents worked. They ran a curb market. I was pretty near spoiled by the time I hit five. All the aunts and uncles and everybody gave me most everything I wanted. I decided being a bastard wasn't so bad after all.

There were different sections of town and I explored all of them. There was the downtown part with all the stores, movie houses, cafes, dance halls, and the city auditorium. My favorite store was Sears and Roebuck. They had the biggest and best toy department I have ever seen, and when you walked in there was a certain smell, a glorious smell of all those toys, wooden tinker toys, electric trains, Red Ryder BB guns, toy metal trucks and cars and planes, cars you could peddle, toy tractors, cowboy outfits, red scooters and bicycles, and six shooters that would shoot caps. What a wonderful place.

Then there were the movie houses, the Strand, the Tidville, the Charles, the Empire, and the Paramount, which was the biggest and best. They all smelled the same, popcorn and candy. The dance halls were forbidden territory, I could only look through the windows and watch the older people jump around and get tired and then have to hold one another up. The city auditorium was where they had all the get togethers.

All the colored people would get together and then all the white people would get together. I would go to all of the get togethers. I had more fun when the colored people would get together, cause they would shout and sing and clap their hands. There were times when I wished I was colored, but being a bastard had its advantages.

There were other sections of town where all the colored people stayed and ran their businesses, and there was one movie house there called the Pekin Theater. I would go there sometimes, but would have to sit in the balcony cause I was white. I told them I was a white bastard, but they would just laugh, and I still had to sit in the balcony.

The red light district was on the north and west side of town. There wasn't much going on in this section, nothing but a bunch of women sitting on U the front porches trying to look pretty. They told me I should come back when I was older. We moved to the country before I got older and I never did get a chance to go back. I don't think I would have liked just sitting on the front porch anyway.

We moved to the country before my sixth birthday. I sure missed the city for a while, but soon found the country just as interesting as the city. But that's another story.

WHERE BABY CALVES COME FROM

John Dave (Pete) Fuller

As a young child, growing up on a farm provided a variety of interesting experiences, many of them educational. Children growing up in the city miss an awful lot. In fact, I think all kids should have to spend at least some of their summers on the farm. You really haven't lived 'til you've swung out of the top of a sweetgum tree, ate sour grass on a hot summer day, smoked cross vines, fished for catfish or brim or perch, rode calves in a plowed field, hunted squirrel on a brisk fall morn, and......I could go on and on.

What I was really interested in as a young boy was cows. They were fascinating animals. They would graze in the field and then lay down in the shade and chew and chew on the grass they had eaten. Adults called it chewing on their cud (I guess that's the way you spell it). Anyway, at the time I didn't know cows had more than one stomach, some for storing food and some for digesting it.

I often wondered why some cows had horns and some didn't, or why some were spotted, some were brown, and some were black and had long tongues that were like sandpaper. I also wondered why the bulls (the male cows) kept trying to ride the female cows (the heifers). It was a mystery to me, and what the adults told me didn't make any sense. They said they were breeding, whatever that meant.

Anyway, the baby calves and I had a lot of fun together. They would chase me and I would turn around and chase them. They would butt me and I would try to ride them, not like the bull though. We had a great time together.

I was always finding the little suckers hiding out in the high grass, close to an old stump way out in the back side of the pasture. In fact, almost every calf I found was near some old stump. Well, I thought, maybe that's where they come from. Yep, it had to be. Baby calves came from old stumps out in the fields and woods, because I always found them there. I also noticed that if a bull was riding a cow day after day, it wasn't long 'til I would find a calf by a stump, and that calf would follow the same cow that the ole bull was a ridin'. That heifer would let the calf suck her teats 'til he was too big to and had to start eating grass. I was told he got milk from those teats. Cows were strange creatures.

Song: Ole MacDonald Had a Farm

THE *BOUNCER* (25 to 3 Fight)

John Dave (Pete) Fuller

It was a warm June night. I had just opened the dance hall, a long frame building with screen windows all the way around on both sides and the front. There was a side entrance on the left side in the back. Double doors were at the front entrance. The only light was furnished by a 1950 Wurlitzer juke box and a small 40 watt light bulb. Dancers don't like much light. The floor was worn slick by dancing shoes and sand tracked in from the outside. There was a long bench attached to the right wall to sit on, and three support posts spaced down the middle. The building had a tin roof and a huge squirrel cage fan in one corner to help cool the dancers down. It was a normal Friday night, starting out slow, but couples began to filter in one by one. A few stags were mixed in with the couples.

About eight o'clock I was getting hungry and things were running smooth, so I ran up to the sandwich shop and picked up my usual snack: a barbecue, a hamburger, a hot dog, a 16 ounce R.C. cola, some potato chips, and two moon pies for desert. I was a growing boy and needed nourishment. I had been swimming most of the day.

I returned to the dance hall with my food and sat down on the long bench in the corner. About the time I finished my snack three guys came in I knew, Tommy Davis, quarterback on the Holtville High School football team, Barney Reynolds, a three-hundred pound guard on the same team, and Bud Oats, who was from Wetumpka.

Tommy Davis and Bud Oats immediately began dancing and Barney sat down on the bench beside me and struck up a conversation. We talked for about 15 minutes and I had to excuse myself to mull around the dance floor and outside to check and make sure nobody was drinking or doing anything they weren't supposed to be doing. I noticed the house was beginning to fill up. I checked out all the corners and walked to the front entrance and stood in the doorway so I could see the whole dance floor.

It was then I noticed a lot of—about 20 or 25—stags beginning to float in. I did not recognize any of them, and I began to get an uneasy feeling. They all crowded into the doorway, shoving as they came in. I sensed something going down. I was right. Immediately somebody busted out the light. Girls screamed, cussing began, and grunts and groans heard, all in total darkness. Somebody had pulled the jukebox plug. A fight had started.

It took me about five seconds to run 75 yards to the swimming pool to get my dad. We ran back to the dance hall in about ten seconds. My dad wasn't as fast as me. He was forty years older than me. When we got to the dance hall front door my dad whipped out his blackjack. It was about 12 inches long and had a double handle you could wrap around your hand, and a big end filled with mustard seed and sand. It was designed to knock you out and not cut you.

My dad told me to grab the big stick wedged on the right side of the screen door to prop it back. It was made out of hickory and about five feet long. It was stout. He told me to go in swinging and hit anything moving, but watch out for him. He always wore a big Stetson hat, so that was not a problem.

My eyes had adjusted to the dark. I waded in, hitting anybody standing up. All the girls had run out the back and front doors. Every time I hit somebody he would go down. Two guys had somebody down on the floor slugging' him. I knocked the two off him. It was Bud Oats. He was bleeding. Barney Reynolds was backed into a corner and plastering anybody who came at him. By now my dad had laid out quite a few and told me to start dragin' them out the door. Tommy Davis had been beat up pretty bad. Barney Reynolds didn't have a scratch.

When everything had cooled down we learned that about 25 boys from West End in Montgomery had come to whip up on Davis, Oats and Reynolds. That was one big fist fight, but 25 to 3 was not good odds. It took one 55-year-old man and a 14-year-old kid with a hickory stick to even the odds.

After we had emptied the dance hall and locked it up, my dad and me were walking back to the pool. Three boys from West End were walking behind us. One of them hollered at my dad and said, "Ole man, you're not so tough. I think I'll just whup your butt. You ain't nothin' but a sawedoff #!!?X!?#Z! S.O.B."

I wished he hadn't said that. I knew what was coming. My dad whipped out his blackjack and hit the young man right on the bridge of the nose. Blood flew everywhere. The West End boy hit the ground with a thud, out cold. The other two ran.

"If you talk like a man you should be able to take it like a man," said my dad.

That 18-year-old grew up that night.

My dad told me, and some other guy he knew, to take the West End boy out to the road and prop him up by the telephone pole so some of his friends could pick him up. We did.

That was the only fight we ever had at the dance hall or pool. Word got around that my dad and some guy with a hickory stick ran a tight ship. That's me, *The Bouncer.*

LITTLE HENRY, ALIAS "PETE"

John Dave (Pete) Fuller

Everything has to have a beginning, and everything has to have a creator. God created the universe and everything in it, including the earth and all life on this planet. God designed all living species so that they could create their own kind. A male and a female dog can create a baby dog, either male or female, depending on the sperm that docks with the female egg. The first sperm to get to the egg determines the sex, physical and mental characteristics of the infant animal or human. This was the way Little Henry, alias *Pete*, was created.

The year was 1938. A nationwide depression was winding down. Money was tight, especially in L.A.—that's lower Alabama—in the town of Greenville. Farmers were growing cotton, corn, beans, watermelons, squash, collards, and anything to eat and sell to survive. Not too much selling went on because nobody had any money. You could pay for a doctor's visit with a dozen eggs or a mess of collards. It was about this time of year, May, 1938, that God decided that Little Henry, alias Pete, was to be created and then born into the world.

The first thing God had to do was to pick out the man and woman to do the creating, and Little Henry didn't have a say-so in this decision. If he had he might have picked a rich couple, a good-looking couple, a very smart couple, an artistic couple, a movie star couple, a black couple, an Indian couple, a Jewish couple, or a Gentile couple. Well, wouldn't you know it, God didn't even pick a couple at all. He picked a married man and an unmarried seventeen-year-old girl. They were both white Gentiles it seems, because Little Henry was white, with black hair and brown eyes. He had a chicken chest, his navel was off center, one leg was just a little shorter than the other, and he had flat feet. Other than that, he was perfect.

Now Little Henry was created in the height of passion on a warm May Day in 1938. It seems that this married man was sexually attracted to this nicelooking seventeen-year-old girl and one day after school had let out (this man was either a school principal, a coach, or a music teacher), Little Henry was created in one of the empty classrooms, in the principal's office on his desk, or in the gym locker room. Little Henry didn't have a choice in the matter. If he had he probably would have chosen a better place: the podium in the band room, the chemistry lab, the art room, or maybe the bed in the home economics room. Wherever it was Little Henry was created on a day in May, 1938. Only God knows where, the married man, and the seventeen-year-old. Little Henry didn't have a clue.

Now this created several problems, and the married man and the seventeen-year-old had nine months to find a solution to all the problems.

One problem was who would claim Little Henry when he popped out into the world. Creating is one thing. Responsibility is another. Even animals take care of their young. Since Little Henry was created by a married man and an unwed mother, he was considered illegitimate, or a bastard to put it plainly.

The married man didn't want Henry in his family, and the unwed mother didn't have a family since she didn't have a husband, and her mother and father already had a bunch of kids. They didn't need another to feed and have to take care of. There was a depression going on and babies were expensive. Why did God choose to have Little Henry created this way? Well, God didn't choose. A moment of lust and passion did the choosing. God allowed it to happen and Little Henry just happened to be the fastest sperm in the pen. God's law of nature took over and the sperm and the egg joined together and created Little Henry down to the last little toenail.

If nobody claimed Henry, would he be put in an orphan home, or would they just go ahead and abort him? The man didn't seem to care. He was kinda like Fido, who had puppies everywhere within a five-mile radius. The girl felt different. She didn't want to abort, but knew the stigma Henry would have to deal with the rest of his life if he stayed in Greenville after he was born.

Finally, a decision was made. Madge—that was the mother's name—decided to go to another town, have the baby, and put Henry up for adoption. Hopefully, someone would adopt him.

Well, Little Henry lay around for about nine months growing and working on his DNA 'til it was time for him to be born. The big day finally arrived and out popped Little Henry right on schedule, exactly nine months from the day Henry blew out of the starting gate, flew down the Fallopian tube, and beat all of the other wannabees to the finish line. What a race!

Henry opened his eyes only to see some strange creature hovering over him. Henry was immediately introduced to pain, a sharp pain on his back U side. Then this creature lifted a bright, gleaming object over him and proceeded to whittle away on his front side. Henry was beginning to get second thoughts about winning that race. A bad idea. No sooner had the pain stopped and Henry had settled down another creature appeared and started mumblin' and droppin' something all over him. What a strange world!

Well, Henry decided, "I'm here. I might as well make the best of it."

Things did get better. They wrapped Henry up in a warm blanket and fed him a warm liquid.

"Hey! Things are lookin' better all the time. I could get used to this."

Henry was adopted on the third day of his young life in the office of Dr. Black on the corner of Montgomery Street and Molton, on the second floor over the Buster Brown clothing store. Dave and Ecie Fuller adopted him and his name was changed to John Dave Fuller, alias *Pete*. The year was 1939, the month was January. The second race was begun.

HI MOM!

John Dave (Pete) Fuller

Hi mom. I'm part of your life that happened many years ago, a part of your life you may have forgotten or wanted to forget, for in that time and generation things were different from today in so many ways. People dressed different, acted different, and maybe looked different, but were still human beings made in God's image. So, really, they were not much different from people today.

In 1939, during the month of January, I was born in Montgomery, Alabama. I don't know where, perhaps in a hospital or in the back room of Dr. Black's office (he was the doctor that brought me into this world). You know the time and place well. You were just seventeen or eighteen, and maybe not ready for motherhood, and the world was not ready for me. The world frowned on my particular conception, however right or wrong they were. They would not accept the fact that children have been conceived for centuries under similar circumstances and were called illegitimate. Some people even tried to say that Jesus was born out of wedlock—illegitimate, whatever illegitimate means.

I consider myself to be as legitimate as the next fellow. I have a mother and a father. That makes me legitimate. The fact that my mother and father made a mistake doesn't mean I'm not here. Just because society does or did not accept my birth in 1939, and tried to sweep me under the rug, doesn't mean I'm not a living, breathing soul, a living breathing soul needing all the love and care so-called legitimate children receive. To a society that thinks this way, I say to hell with them. God doesn't think that way. God does not turn his back on any child being born in any situation, when, where, or how they were conceived.

Mother I salute you for doing what was necessary in a world so unkind. I know it was difficult, for I have children and grandchildren of my own and would hate to give them away. Though I have never met you, I feel like I have always known you. I still have the knitted shoes and hat, and small pillow you made for me. My foster mother saved them and gave them to me when I was older. I guess you can say I was lucky. I had two mothers.

I want you to know the decision you made at the time was right. You must have known how cruel the world would have been to an illegitimate child in 1939 with no father or mother. You chose not to abort me and not put me in an orphan home, but you found two parents who were willing to take me and give me a good, loving home. Maybe it broke your heart. I hope not, because it was the right decision for me.

The family you gave me raised me well. I haven't wanted for anything. I have children and grandchildren of my own now, many years later. I would that I could meet you and let you tell me about yourself. I would that I could return the favor to you for what you did for me. I know I'll never see you in this lifetime, but will see you in the next life and we can talk. We all can meet together, you, me, my foster parents, my wife, and children, and grandchildren, and friends, and talk for an eternity. I LOVE YOU MOM!

Your Loving Son,
Little Henry

Later in my life I found out who my mother was, though I never met her. I did meet my grandmother. My mother was a nurse and had married an airline pilot. My grandmother told me not to contact her, for it might cause problems in her marriage. I respected her decision. I later learned my mother had developed Alzheimer's Disease. She would not have remembered me anyway. I really would have liked to have seen her just once, but it has not happened.

John D. (Pete) Fuller, alias *Little Henry*

DAVE FULLER
John Dave (Pete) Fuller

The sun had not yet broken the morning sky as the twinkle of a star shown through an occasional hole in the tin roof. As I peered from under several quilts the cold air told me not to get up. I quickly drew my head back under my quilt shell and closed my eyes tightly, wanting to go back to sleep, but someone was stirring in the next room. I didn't have to guess who it was. It was only a matter of time, when.......... DAVE!! COME!!

Grandpa had struck again. I now had a choice. Get up and start a fire, or in about three shakes of an otter's tail a dipper of ice cold well water would be running down my nice warm backside. Considering my choices I quickly hit the floor. The cold air swallowed me completely. I had to get something on in a hurry or frost over. My breath was already hanging in the air longer than normal. Must be about twenty degrees outside I thought. I quickly slid into my half-frozen clothes and made my way to the woodshed. I had cut enough wood yesterday evening to make a good fire, but I needed something to help me get warm. The wood was frozen so I grabbed the axe and started swinging at the wood with the butt end; it was just what I needed to get me warm.

I piled the wood high on my left arm and staggered toward the house yellin' for my brother Delmus to open the door. I always carried too much so I wouldn't have to make two trips, but I usually dropped several sticks between the woodpile and the house, and had to go back anyway. This morning though, I made it all the way to the wood box and didn't drop a stick.

Once I got the old wood stove goin', things warmed up pretty good. It was especially warm around the stack coming out the back. It was fun to drop water on the top of the stove and watch it dance. I guess this old stove probably burned many a stick of wood, and was still goin' strong now.

As the room warmed I knew it was time for breakfast, and afterwards doin' the rest of my chores. As I sat down I knew I'd probably get it for not washing my face, because cold weather and cold water don't mix. Maybe Grand Ma won't notice this morning. She didn't. Now I can enjoy my biscuits, red-eye gravy, fried green *tomaters*, and black coffee. Life ain't so bad after all.

Song: Country Roads

THE PIANO PROBLEM

John Dave (Pete) Fuller

Well, it's Sunday again, and I gotta go to church. The reason for going my parents said was that God worked six days and rested on the seventh. I don't know what going to church has to do with God resting. Maybe he's watching us while he's resting, because when he's workin' he don't have time to watch us. I don't know because I'm only four years old. When I get older I can figure it out.

Anyway, this is a special Sunday. My daddy, my granddaddy, and my Uncle Dave are going to be turned out of church. My daddy and granddaddy got drunk and somebody saw them, so they are going to be turned out of church. My Uncle Dave, who is an elder, is going to be turned out because of a piano problem. This I don't understand because he can't even play the piano.

I don't know if they are going to turn me out; nobody told me if they are. If they turn my daddy out I can't come anyway because we only have one car and my daddy does the driving. I can't reach the steering wheel yet, so I couldn't drive. My mother drives too fast and gets tickets all the time, so I guess we'll just stay home. Maybe God can watch us at home.

The church building is full of people now, and they are all dressed up in their Sunday clothes. These are clothes you only wear on Sunday. I heard somebody say they were *Sunday-Go-To-Meetin'* clothes. All the women have on hats. My aunt Rosie, Uncle Dave's wife, likes hats. She makes up her own. I never know what she'll be wearing from one Sunday to the next. All the men wear suits if they have one, especially the preacher and the elders. Some of the men wear new overalls and a white shirt. I just wear whatever they put on me.

When we all get seated and get quiet, Mr. Bledsoe gets up front and says a few words, announcing a number in a song book and starting everybody singing. Sometimes my mother will find the song in my book so I can sing along. I make up my own words, because I can't read the words in the book. Sometimes my words last longer than the other words, and when everyone else is finished I keep on singing. Everybody must like it because they all turn and look at me, smiling. God must have liked it too. He never complained. They said God was there, but I don't know where he sat. I never did see him. Once I thought I saw God sitting with the elders, because someone was sitting with them with a lot of hair, but it turned out to be a visiting preacher. The singing sounded good, and I liked to sing. I guess I enjoyed the singing most of all. I liked Mr. Bledsoe too. He was nice.

Well, anyway, we all sang a bunch of songs, and then someone got up and prayed. We all close our eyes while the prayer is being prayed. Sometimes the prayer is real long and I go to sleep, but wake up when they sing another song.

After the singing and praying the preacher gets up to preach. He usually preaches a long time, and I get sleepy again and fall asleep, but wake up when he shouts and bangs on the preacher stand. God may get sleepy too, because the preacher don't know when to stop sometimes.

After the preacher finishes preaching, everybody sings a song called the invitation song, and anybody who wants to can go up and talk to the preacher. They might ask him to let them back into the church after telling him that they will do better. The preacher don't tell what they have done, but everybody already knows, cause I hear people talking about what they have done way before they go up to talk to the preacher. Some of the things they have done don't make sense to me: drinking, cussin', fortication, runnin' around on their wife, gossipin', forsaking the assembly, and /lasciviousness. All of these are sins according to the preacher. I guess when I get older I will find out what they are.

It was during this invitation song that my daddy and granddaddy went up to talk to the preacher. I don't know what they talked about, but when they finished the preacher was very happy, and said he was glad these two sinners were willing to change their ways. This was news to me. I didn't know my daddy and granddaddy were sinners. Anyway, they decided not to turn my daddy and granddaddy out for getting drunk. I'm glad because now I won't have to stop gettin' drunk with the other kids in the backyard. I loved spinning around and around 'til I was so drunk I couldn't walk straight, and would fall down. This was such fun.

They did turn my Uncle Dave out though. As soon as they finished talking to my daddy and granddaddy, a man got up. The man was an elder because he had on a suit, wore a necktie, and had grey hair, at least what was left of it. He said that because of the piano problem they would have to turn my uncle out of the church, and he couldn't go there anymore. They didn't even ask God what he thought. I was hoping they would, because I wanted to see Him.

Everything turned out good for us. We all went to another church that was closer to our house. I got to be in a class with a bunch of kids my age. The class was taught by Mrs. Mitchell. We all sang and clapped our hands, and she told us stories about God and Jesus, who was God's son. Nothing was ever said about the piano problem that Uncle Dave had. I guess he'd sold it.

AIR RAIDS

John Dave (Pete) Fuller

In 1942, I was only three-years-old. We lived on Lawrence Street in Montgomery, Alabama. The house we lived in was a two-story wood frame house with a high front porch. Every house on the block was the same: a front living room, kitchen next (you ate in the kitchen), and a back bedroom. There was a long hall on the right side and a bathroom under the stairs. There were more bedrooms upstairs.

Besides the sidewalk and the side alley, one of my favorite places to play was the front porch. Being a three-year-old with a wild imagination, that front porch could be anything from a ship, an airplane, a castle, or, maybe, a Jack Cole transfer truck.

In 1942 a war was ragin' *they* said (*they* were the adults). We were fighting the Japs because they bombed some island called Pearl out in the ocean. Anyway, it made Roosevelt mad and we started fightin'. There was talk about all sorts of things: us being taken over by the Japs, all the men being drafted, the USO, Zeros, Flying Tigers, B-Twenty-Nines, B-TwentyFives, WACS, Marines, Army Air Corps, and submarines. There was even talk about some guy named Hitler. I think his first name was Heil, or Hell, or something like that. There was also something wrong with his right arm. He was always raising it up in the air. I don't think he could bend it very well. Hitler was not like the Japs. They were little and had funny-looking eyes, and always wore funny little caps. Hitler didn't wear a cap, but something was wrong with his top lip.

Sometimes during the day sirens would start screaming and everybody would go inside the house. If it was night we'd go inside the house and cut off all the lights. They said the Japs would be coming in their Zeros; they would be coming in the sky. This was called an air raid, and if we saw 'em we could shoot 'em down with our guns.

Well, the only gun I had was an old Daisy BB gun, and I was not allowed to U have BBs, but I found some and saved them for the air raids. After everybody had gone inside I'd slip out on the front porch and take my BB gun, load it, and be on the lookout for Zeros. I'd never seen one, but I figured they would be small with a little, funny-looking man sitting inside with a cap on. I knew Hitler couldn't fly, with his arm being straight you know, and he was probably too big to get in one of those little Zeros.

I spent many an afternoon on our front porch looking for Zeros during the air raids. I shot at a few, but most of them turned out to be pigeons. If I hit any I didn't know it. I think I needed a bigger gun.

Song: Wild Blue Yonder (Air Force song)

JAMES LEE "SNOKIE" MULDER

John Dave (Pete) Fuller

In my twelve years of elementary and high school there were many colorful characters. *Snokie* Mulder was one of those characters. His character could fit into any movie script, as a sidekick to a Western star, a member of the *East Side Gang* of teenagers, or just the community good-ole-boy.

Snokie joined the football team during my sophomore year. He didn't look like a football player. He was skinny. Soaking wet he wouldn't weigh 145 pounds, but could run like a deer, smooth and fast. Yet he was easy to tackle. If he ever got one step ahead of you, catching him was impossible.

Nothing seemed to bother *Snokie*. If he made a mistake, so what. Everybody makes mistakes. Life is filled with mistakes.

One Friday night the football team had an away game and everybody was responsible for packing their equipment and loading it on the equipment truck. When we arrived and were all dressing for the game, *Snokie* realized that he had forgotten to bring white socks, and nobody had an extra pair for *Snokie*. Did that bother him? Would the coach get mad? No problem!! *Snokie* wrapped his ankles with toilet paper and taped the paper to his legs. During the game some of the tape came loose and when he would run the paper and tape would flap behind him. It was a funny sight. The fans got a good laugh. Coach got a little upset. *Snokie* looked like Mercury, the god of speed. Life went on.

On another night we were playing at home and *Snokie* was playing defensive halfback. Between snaps Snokie would relax by standing crosslegged and picking his nose. Some of the other players told *Snokie* to stop picking his nose, but this didn't bother him a bit. He did have on socks.

Well, *Snokie* left after the tenth grade. His family moved up north, and if *Snokie* graduated nobody knew. Several years later we heard that *Snokie* was killed in a car accident while driving to work one night. *Snokie* will be missed, and when you get to heaven you can look for *Snokie*. He will be the most relaxed person there.

SCHOOLYARD FOOTBALL

John Dave (Pete) Fuller

Let the game begin. Every day at recess was kickoff time. There was only one quarter of play from the beginning of recess 'til the end, and no timeouts. The equipment was minimal: one football, which belonged to one of the players. There were no pads, no helmets. Some wore street clothes or no shoes, and tear away shirts—the buttons ripped off easy. Since the playing field was the school yard and was not marked off, a first down was either three completed passes or ten yards, marked off by a rock, or can, or whatever was available.

Out of bounds was a matter of opinion and usually included the whole playground, minus the swings, the seesaws, the sidewalks, and the buildings. There were no referees, and unnecessary roughness was the order of the day. If you got injured you just got out of everybody's way 'ti you were ready to play again.

The number of players was not important. Everybody who wanted to play, played. The plays were simple. A center snapped the ball to one person, who either passed or ran the ball until tackled. Anybody was eligible for a pass or a handoff to run the ball.

The defense was simple. Everybody tackled the ball carrier, even if you had to run over one or two players to get to him. The runner was down when he hit the ground, and as long as he was standing he was fair game. You could hit him with your shoulder, or grab him by the leg, arm, neck, foot, or anything you could get hold of to bring him down. The only thing not legal was sluggin'. If this happened the *sluggor* and the *sluggee* usually wound up sluggin' it out on the sidelines, which usually ended the game if the teacher saw the fight (the teachers usually sat in a little circle in the corner of the playground and rarely got involved in our play), and a trip to the principal's office was necessary. Both parties usually got their butts whipped, so sluggin' was rare. Besides, why slug the ball carrier when you could run over him, slam him to the ground, or hold him by the leg 'til somebody else ran over him.

Gang tacklin' was the order of the day. There was this big fifth grader who was hard to bring down, it usually taking four or five to tackle him. The defense usually keyed on him every play, because he usually ran the ball every play. Passing was minimal, and if you were brave enough to catch the ball you were usually mobbed by the whole defense. Nobody kicked field goals because there were no goal posts. The big kid usually drug half the defense over the goal line for the extra point.

Well, after playin' school yard football in the fourth, fifth, sixth, seventh, and eight grade I was finally old enough to go out for the high school team in the ninth grade. I could not believe it. Why, we got to put on helmets, shoulder pads, thigh pads, hip pads, knee pads, rib pads, and this strange-looking device called an athletic supporter, which I really didn't need. I forgot to mention we also got to wear shoes with little black knobs on the bottom called cleats, and had a face guard to protect your nose and teeth. After I got used to all that protection, I found out you could knock down the big kid with ease. By the way, I finally did need that athletic supporter when I got a little older.

Song: Mr. Touchdown

JAIL TIME FOR A TEN-YEAR-OLD?

John Dave (Pete) Fuller

On a cool fall day in 1950 I was visiting my three cousins in Pine Level, Alabama. Now Pine Level was located somewhere in the middle of nowhere. In other words, it was out in the sticks. For some strange reason we were all bored, so we decided to play some football. We chose up sides and I was the last one chosen, since I was the smallest and just visiting.

The game began and everything was going pretty well 'til some of the larger boys began to make fun of me for some strange reason. They would only let me block and I wasn't allowed to pass, run, or kick the ball, but I accepted it and was content with my fate 'til they started pickin' on me. It was beginning to get under my skin.

As the game wore on and the raggin' got worse, I got madder and madder, 'til I decided to take matters in my own hand. I was only a blocker, but I could tackle if I had the chance. I waited and waited and finally got a shot at one of my cousins. I think he thought he could run over me, but I had different ideas. All of a sudden I developed tunnel vision and all I could see was my cousin running toward me. I decided to run over him. I lunged forward and hit him between his knees and waist with my right shoulder, and wrapped my arms around his legs. There was a thud and a strange cracking sound. My cousin didn't get up. A silence fell over the crowd. Nobody said a word. My cousin just lay there in obvious pain.

Well, I was in trouble. It seems my cousin's leg was broken and we had to rush him to Fitts-Hill Hospital in Montgomery, Alabama. My dad and my aunt and granddad took my cousin to the hospital. I just kind of tagged along. My other cousins told me I might be put in jail for what I had done. I paced up and down this long hall for about an hour.

Finally, my dad came and got me, and told me they had put a cast on my cousin's leg, from his ankle to his hip, and it would stay on for six months. He also told me that football was over for me, and that he would not allow me to play that game anymore. I thought "What about jail time," but didn't say anything. I decided to leave well-enough alone.

My cousin got better and six months later the cast was removed. It would be two years before I was allowed to play any more football. I finally convinced my dad to allow me to try out for the Blue Hornet football team for seventh and eighth graders.

BLUE HORNET FOOTBALL

John Dave (Pete) Fuller

The Blue Hornet football team practiced after school every day down by the ice house, and the old L & N Depot by the Methodist church. The team was sponsored by the church. You had to furnish your own equipment. They provided the transportation to the game, the coach, Billy Moore, and a blue and white jersey.

Since my dad finally let me play football, he took me to a sporting goods store and bought me all of my equipment. It didn't do me any good the first year cause I sat on the bench. I think I played one play in one game. All I remember is that the other team was called the Red Raiders and they looked huge in their red jerseys.

The second year was the year for our Blue Hornet team. We were undefeated that year. We beat every team in our league except one. We tied that team 7 to 7 and went on to play for the city championship in Crampton Bowl in Montgomery.

Our team was the only team not in the city limits of Montgomery. We were considered outcasts, a group of country hicks. There were no stars on our team. We all worked together to try to win. It didn't matter to us who scored the touchdowns. I guess we were all a bunch of unsung heroes who just played the game for fun. There was no pressure to win, but we usually found a way to win.

In the championship game we played Capitol Chevrolet, a team we beat in the regular season, but they had beat the team we tied. The team we tied had lost one other game, so were not bowl eligible. We were the only undefeated team in the league.

The championship game ended in a 0 to 0 tie. We thought we had won the city championship, but the powers that be, namely the officials of the league, proclaimed Capitol Chevrolet the winner. They said they had picked up one more first down than we had, thus were declared the winner of the game. Where did that rule come from, and who made that decision? We were the only undefeated team, but did not win the championship because of a rule that appeared out of nowhere.

You decide who the real winner was. It didn't bother us, we knew who the real winner was. Besides, we didn't have a trophy case to put the trophy in. It was a cheap looking trophy anyway, and our trophy was our undefeated season. Not bad for a bunch of country hicks!

Alternate ending

The championship game ended in a 0 to 0 tie. We thought we had won the city championship because we had not lost a game but tied two and we had beaten Captiol Chevrolet during the regular season, but the powers that be, namely the officials of the league, proclaimed Capitol Chevrolet the winner. They said they had picked up one more first down than we had, thus were declared the winner of the game. Where did that rule come from, and who made that decision? We were the only undefeated team, but did not win the championship because of a rule that appeared out of nowhere.

You decide who the real winner was. It didn't bother us too much, we knew who the real winner was. Besides, we didn't have a trophy case to put the trophy in anyway, and it was a cheap looking trophy. Our trophy was our undefeated season. Not bad for a bunch of country hicks! What do you think?

DEHORNING COWS

John Dave (Pete) Fuller

Growing up on a farm provides many opportunities to learn about nature and animals. Every animal is treated differently. Some young calves and young pigs have to be cut (a quick way to keep some from becoming a father) and horses have to be shoed (shod) with metal shoes. Some cows have to be dehorned to keep them from hooking one another. Sometimes we would dehorn only one, but, usually, more than one.

Now there's an art to dehorning, but first they have to be rounded up. The bad ones have to be driven in a catch lot with a quarter horse, but some come up if you call them. Once you get them in the lot the real work begins. One person is in charge of packin' the holes in the cow's head with cotton and tar after the horns have been cut off. Someone else has to run 5 the cows into the shute, and then someone operates a device that catches the cow's neck to hold the cow still. My job was to operate the dehorner, a large guillotine-looking device with sharp blades that came together and whacked off the horn.

You had to be careful to make sure you got the device close down to the head so as to get all of the horn. You didn't want to leave a nub. I always stood on the sides of the shute and straddled the cow's head. It was important for whoever was holding the head to keep it still. The cow could do a lot of damage with those horns if her head was allowed to lash sideways and up and down. I didn't want to be made a eunuch at my age.

Anyway, when the cow was ready I straddled her head, put the dehorner over one horn and clamped down the handles. There was a loud crunch, the horn dropped off, a stream of blood shot upward, and if I was lucky it only hit me on my chest and not in my face.

Very quickly you had to open the blades and whack off the other horn amidst spurting blood, cotton and tar being packed in the holes, and the cow bellowing at the top of her lungs. When they let her go she slung blood, tar and spit all over everybody within a five foot circle.

Well, the first one was done, only nine more to go. Someone asked me if I hurt the cow. I don't know. I've never been dehorned. Maybe you should ask the cow.

LIFE IN THE FAST LANE

John Dave (Pete) Fuller

It was a warm June morning as I crawled out of bed. I didn't bother to put on my clothes. I slid into my bathing suit and headed for the swimming pool. My daddy had built and operated a public pool called Willow Springs, and one of my jobs was to check for snakes and dip off any leaves that had fell in the pool overnight. I also got to keep any money I found on the bottom that someone had lost the day before. Some mornings I would find a dollar or more in the deep end. I had to dive down about ten feet to pick it up, but to a ten year old that was big money.

After dippin' off the leaves and checkin' for snakes I had to clean the bath houses next. I usually found a little money under the wood lattices in the mens' side, but hardly ever in the ladies' side. The mens' side was always the biggest mess and smelled the worst. The ladies' side never had much trash on the floor and always smelled slightly of perfume. Women were better housekeepers than men.

Both men and women though, like to write on the bath house walls. The women used lipstick to write with and wrote of love and boyfriends. The men used pencils or carved with a knife to leave their messages. Some were funny but most were dirty.

One funny one was written over the toilet: *PLEASE FLUSH. WETUMPKA NEEDS WATER.* Well, I thought it was funny. My mother didn't. Some included a girl's name and phone number, and said to call for a good time. I called one or two, but always got a busy signal. I guess they were busy having a good time.

After cleanin' the bath house, my next job was to sweep the sandwich shop and the dance hall. I liked to do the dance hall 'cause I would play a few records on the Rockola and dance with my broom. It took me longer to sweep the dance hall 'cause me and that broom could sure cut a rug. There were a lot of cigarette butts on the floor and sometimes I would save a few and strip off the paper, leaving only the tobacco to use in my corn cob pipe. I would slip around every now and then and smoke my pipe. I stopped this after a while, because it burned my tongue and tasted bad.

I had to keep the grass cut and about once a week I cranked up the ole Briggs and Stratton and had at it, the grass I mean. One day I was cuttin' grass in our front yard when a friend of mine came by riding a Whizzer motorbike. He stopped and we talked a while, and he asked me if I wanted to ride his motorbike. I had never ridden a motorbike before, but it looked easy, so I said yes. He cranked it up and I crawled on the seat, and grabbed the handlebars. There were two levers on the right side of the handlebars. One gave it the gas and the other cut the gas off. There were no brakes. You just cut off the gas and coasted to a stop. Off I went down the road to the swimming pool. I gave it some gas and picked up speed. The trees were whizzin' by. I thought I'd better slow this rig down. I pushed the cut-off lever. The bike got faster. Everything became a blur. I pushed again. Faster! The trees zipped by. I thought this is a dead end road. It ended at the dance hall. I looked up and the sandwich shop was coming up fast. The dance hall was next. My mother came running out the side door yelling, "Jump son! Jump!"

The dance hall lay dead ahead, and a high dirt bank on the left. I turned left and jumped off the bike. The bike hit the bank with a thud and I tumbled end over end several times, barely missing a car. Someone picked me up off the ground. I walked over to the bike. It didn't look good. The gas tank was knocked off and the front wheel was bent. About that time my friend ran up. He had a sick look on his face. I felt stupid and bad. I kept pushin' the trottle instead of pullin' the cut-off valve. A minor mistake caused a major problem. We put the bike back together and my mother treated us to hotdogs and R.C.s. I bid my friend goodbye and got back to cuttin' grass. He left, pushin' his motor bike back home. So much for life in the fast lane.

Song: Dead Man's Curve

COUNTRY MARRIAGE

John Dave (Pete) Fuller

If you live in the country and get married, it's different from the city. Course country life is different from city life in just about every way. The foods different, the work is different, you go to bed at a different time, you get up at a different time, and you walk to school if you go. Life is slower and, well, it's all different.

Now marriage in the country starts out with a courtship and gradually works its way to the marriage altar. The courtship begins with the boy and girl kind of looking out the corner of their eye at each other and then looking off the other way, not wantin' the other to know they are lookin' at 'em. Finally, after they both realize they are actually lookin' at each other, then they meet somewhere in a secret place and just stare at one another. Finally, one gets the courage to speak.

"Hi," one says, and after a long pause the other one says something. "Hi!"

That's pretty much the conversation for the first meeting, and they both leave knowing that they'll meet again some other time, but the same place. This goes on for several weeks and the conversation picks up, and several more words are added. Finally, everybody in the community knows about this relationship and the couple don't have to hide it anymore.

Thus begins the second stage of this here relationship. The boy goes over to the girl's house after asking her daddy if he can court his daughter. I guess this would be called a date in city language. Anyway, everybody knows the couple are sweet on each other. The date consists of just sittin' on the front porch, just swingin' in the swing and talking. This goes on 'dl her daddy says it's time for him to go home. You do not argue with her daddy. Besides, he might turn out to be your daddy-in-law.

These relationships usually get around to holding' hands, except one girl broke up a relationship 'cause after holding' hands one night she knew for sure she was pregnant and that was it. Course she never did have a baby.

After all the courting' is done then comes marriage. Sometimes this can last a year, unless of course uncontrollable circumstances move the date up a bit, like the arrival of a third party.

Marriage celebrations can last a day or two with a lot of fiddling and dancing before and after the ceremony. There is also much planning going on about how to play tricks on the newlyweds. Since there were not many cars and the honeymooners would not leave the community, there was not a lot that could be done. There was no such thing as a bachelor party, no bridal showers to speak of, so we had to use our imagination to come up with some tricks to play on the newlyweds.

One favorite trick was to tie a black nylon fishing line to the newlywed's bed springs, run it through a crack in the floor—most of the houses were built off the ground and had cracks in the floor—and through a swivel under the house. Then the line was run to another swivel, about thirty or forty feet in woods behind the house, and attached to a cowbell hanging' freely so it would clang if the bedsprings moved up and down. If everything was installed right then four or five of us boys would sit around the bell right after sundown on the honeymoon night waiting' for the cows to come home. We were usually not disappointed and sometimes the bell would ring fast, and sometimes it would ring slowly, and sometimes the string would break. The newlyweds never seemed to hear the bell.

THE DAY DAVE FULLER WAS BORN
(as told by Delmus Fuller)

John Dave (Pete) Fuller

It was a cold blustery morning. It was February 2nd, 1898, Ground Hog Day. The wind was beating up on the sweetgum trees on the gully hillside. The sky was overcast and grey. If the sun was going to come up it had better hurry. The clouds were rolling in from the southwest. It was either going to rain or snow. The old ground hog was probably going to sleep in this cold morning.

Everybody was already up and stirring, 'cause there was going to be a new addition to our family. Janie, my mother, was ready to give birth. The midwife had been called for, but had not arrived. I decided to put on my overalls and go sit on the front porch and look for Cat, the midwife, coming up the gully trail.

Our house was a four room *dogtrot* house. The *dogtrot* part was closed in with a front door and the long hall to the back door was also closed. We had a small back porch built around our well. Our outhouse was about 100 feet from our back door. Course it moved from year to year depending on the visits.

It was cold on the porch 'cause the wind was blowing up the gully. I wanted to be the first one to see Cat coming up the trail, so I sat there shivering. As daylight slowly peeked through the trees the branches formed all kinds of shapes. You were limited only by your imagination.

I sat wondering if the baby was going to be a boy or girl. I was hoping for a baby brother to help with the chores—you know, milking cows, chopping wood, plowing mules, and drawing up well water. If it was a girl she would help with the women chores, like cooking, washing dishes, making beds, sweeping, and mending clothes. I was praying for a brother.

I noticed some movement down on the trail. The daylight was brighter now and I could barely make out the outline of someone coming up the trail. It was a big outline, so it had to be Cat, 'cause she was a big woman.

It was Cat. I could hear her singing, *Swing low sweet chariot, coming for to carry me home,* as she bounced up the trail.

When Cat got in the house she took over.

"Boil plenty of water, get out some clean sheets, and get me some alcohol. I'll need plenty of light, and some clean blankets to wrap the baby in. Stay out of my way men, 'cause this is a woman's job."

The time grew near. I could hear my mother's voice moaning, and, occasionally, a short scream. There was one loud scream and then silence. Cat came out of the bedroom, sweat rolling down her brow, holding a bundle in her arms.

"It's a boy," she said. "What 'cha gonna name him?"

"Hot dog! I got me a helper!"

We called him Dave.

DON'T MESS WITH ECIE

John Dave (Pete) Fuller

It was a warm June Tuesday night. The tree frogs were croaking back and forth to one another, their throats bulging with each croak. It was about nine o'clock and there were several swimmers playing around in the swimming pool. Closing time for the pool was ten and everything was winding down. My mother was busy getting the sandwich shop ready for Wednesday. I had already burned the trash and was taking it easy sittin' by the pool with my daddy and one other friend swapping tall tales. As the time past the tales got longer.

My daddy had just finished a tale about his stint in the Army during World War I when a car pulled up and parked by the pool office. Four teenagers crawled out talking loud and cursing. They sauntered up to the entrance gate and my daddy immediately stopped them. I recognized one of them as Cameron Mahoney, a rowdy eighteen-year-old who considered himself a muscle man. They all reeked of beer. My daddy told them they would have to leave, because he did not allow drinking and cussing. He ran a family operation. Mahoney had a beer can in his hand, which he crushed with one hand to show his muscle power. The can was a Pabst Blue Ribbon can, 1950 vintage, and made out of heavy tin. Mahoney cussed again, calling my daddy a sawed-off S.O.B., and asking who was big enough to make them leave. I knew there was going to be trouble.

My daddy usually carried a blackjack in his right pocket. I looked and there was no bulge there. He had already retired the blackjack and left it under the register in the sandwich shop. I thought to myself, this could get serious.

My mother walked up from the sandwich shop about this time and repeated what my daddy had said: "You boys will have to leave." Now my mother was not a frail woman. You could say she was big-boned and on the stout side.

"Bitch," Mahoney told my mother. "Ain't no woman gonna tell me what to do!"

He immediately swung and hit her in the face on her right jaw, and took a fighting stance. My mother's head reeled backwards about six inches, but strained up quickly. In one quick motion she reached in her rolled down stocking, whipped out my daddy's blackjack with her left hand, and hit Mahoney on the right side of his head. He spun backwards and fell in the pool, knocked out cold.

My mother then proceeded to attack the other three. She hit one a glancing blow and knocked him to his knees. The other two ran for the car. In the meantime my father had called the sheriff.

Mahoney was still in the pool out cold and somebody yelled, "He'll drown if you don't get him out."

"Let him drown," my mother said. "It'll save the taxpayers a lot of money."

But someone fished him out anyway. They drug him to the car and threw him in the back seat.

After calling the sheriff my father had gotten his .38 Smith & Wesson and was walking toward the car. One teenager jumped in the driver's seat, cranked her up, and they took off. One of Mahoney's legs was hanging out the back window. The car disappeared into the June night.

No sooner had the teenagers left the sheriff drove up. He just kept getting out of the car. He was 6'5", wore a white Stetson, and packed a 38.

"Ya'll need any help?" he asked.

My mother looked him in the eye and said, "It wasn't nothing we couldn't handle Sheriff. Would you like a cold R.C.?"

"Don't mind if I do Ecie," the sheriff replied. "Make that a double."

SLOPPIN' HOGS

John Dave (Pete) Fuller

It was 1947 and I was about six-years-old. We lived on a farm in Elmore County, Alabama. My family truck farmed and raised cattle, chickens, guineas, and hogs. About three times a week we got up early and traveled to the big city of Montgomery, Alabama. We went there to pick up the slop to feed the hogs. Now slop was just left over food that the cafes would throw away. We left a 55 gallon drum in the kitchen and the cooks and waitresses would dump the leftover food in the drum. They also dumped shot bottles (small whiskey bottles containing one shot), an occasional dish, knife, fork, and spoon. All of this was mixed together with the food.

We would try to get there early before a lot of people were eating, but usually there were plenty of people there every morning. The two main cafes were the Sheridan and the Exchange Hotel Cafe. There were plenty of other small ones. We would wheel in an empty drum and wheel out a full one on our hand truck, a two-wheel device with handles. This was easier than having to carry the drum. We usually got in and out pretty quick unless some drunk wanted to talk. Some people never sobered up, and usually there was one in every cafe. They seemed to be attracted to the slop. I think they smelled the whiskey that was left over from the shot bottles mixed in with the slop. The slop did have a certain odor about it. Slop smells the same the world over.

After we had made all of our stops we headed back to the farm to slop the hogs. We usually kept about 40 or 50 hogs at a time. We had a mixture of saws (female) and boars (male) hogs. You could tell the difference between them by the two rows of teats hanging down under the saws. There were enough teats to take care of a big litter of little pigs. Some of the hogs were huge, weighing maybe 200 pounds and up. You didn't want to tangle with one.

We fed the hogs at the bottom of a small bluff where there was about a ten-foot dropoff. We had to back our 1942 red Ford pickup right up to the edge of the bluff in order to dump the slop. The hogs were always there waitin' on us, squealin', snortin', and pushing one another to get under the bluff so the slop would fall on them.

One of my jobs was to jump out of the truck, let down the tailgate, and scotch both back tires with a brick. I had to make sure the truck didn't back to far and fall over the bluff. Once the tires were scotched we dumped the slop on top of the hogs. They loved it. You never heard so much squealing in all your life. They were in hog heaven. Sometimes I felt like joining them, but I didn't.

Once we emptied the drums we had to go wash them out with hot water. They had to be clean so the cafe would let us bring them into the kitchen. Once the drums were clean we were ready for another run another day. The hogs had to be slopped rain or shine, cold or hot.

On one cold morning in February everything was frozen over. The roads were slippery, even the ground was frozen. When my mother, who happened to be driving this cold morning, was backing up to the gulley, I had already jumped out, opened the tailgate, and was about to put one brick under the rear tire. My hands were real cold and numb. I reached down and placed the brick behind the tire. The truck slid backwards and up on the brick with my finger caught in between the brick and the tire. I yelled and the truck stopped. I couldn't move. My finger was stuck. My mother got out of the truck wondering what was wrong. She saw what had happened and got back in the truck, cranked it up, and pulled slowly off my finger. My finger was mashed flat. It didn't hurt, but it was really flat, about 1/8 of an inch. I could have used it to dip up my food with.

My parents took me back to our house, where they got some kerosene and had me soak my flattened finger for about an hour. My finger popped right back to normal. I guess I'll have to use a fork and spoon now like everybody else.

ME AND GOAT

John Dave (Pete) Fuller

When I was about five we moved from the city to the country. My daddy decided to become a farmer and raise cattle, pigs, and chickens and grow vegetables to sell at the farmer's market. He also bought me a goat, a little wagon, and harness to hitch goat to the wagon. I don't know if goat was a male or female. All I know was goat was mean and ornery.

Every time we tried to hitch goat up to the wagon he would try to butt you, and if he hit you from behind it would knock you down. Sometimes it took my daddy, mother and me to hitch him up. His horns were curved back over his head and he didn't like anyone touching his horns. He didn't smell very good if you were downwind of him. I usually had to take a bath after playing with him, so I wouldn't smell like a goat.

One summer day I was out driving goat, who was especially ornery. He wanted to go the opposite way I wanted him to go. I finally convinced him to go my way and everything was going smoothly. Round and round the house we would go. I was having a ball playing the wagon master when we passed our seven beehives a little too close, and one of the bee warriors dive-bombed the goat. He hit him right between the eyes. Goat was never one to back away from a fight. After shaking off the bee from his head, he made a beeline for the nearest hive and butted it over. Suddenly a dark cloud arose from the hive. The cloud turned into little bees with nothing on their little bee minds but revenge. They hit me and goat with everything they had, left flank, right flank, rear flank, and frontal flank. They got in my ears, in my hair, down my shirt, in my pants, and anywhere else they could find. My mother saw what was happening and ran to our aid, but by this time my goat had counterattacked and knocked over two more hives. More clouds, more bees. They covered my mother. She grabbed me and pulled me out of my wagon, swattin' bees all the time. We finally got inside the house with some uninvited bees.

My mother managed to swat them with an old newspaper. Dead bees everywhere.

Down by the beehives goat had finished off all the hives, knocking down all seven, and finally high tailing it for the woods. We found him later that day with nothing but the harness on. My wagon was scattered everywhere, a wheel here, a wheel there, a seat here, and the tailgate was in the branch. Goat was covered with dead bees still clinging to his hair.

I was covered with bee stings, and so was my mother. Dead bees were all in her hair. They were in my ears, and when I took off my pants dead bees fell to the floor.

All the bee stingers had to be pulled out of our skin with tweezers. When bees sting, it's a death blow for them. They lose their stinger and part of their tail.

The remedy for bee stings in the country is tobacco juice, so my mother chewed up some tobacco and put little chunks on all my stings. I had brown tobacco spots all over my body, even in places you wouldn't believe. I smelled like tobacco juice and goat. I hurt all over.

Me and goat survived the stings. My daddy made me another wagon and patched goat's harness. I still like to take goat for a drive around the house, but goat won't go near anything that even looks like a beehive, and smoke clouds make me nervous.

Song: Flight of the Bumble Bee

SEARS AND ROEBUCK TAUGHT ME HOW TO READ

John Dave (Pete) Fuller

Living in the country as a young boy was an experience to remember. City livin' was okay, but the country was better. Things were different in the country. The people talked different, the smells were different, time seemed to stand still. There was swimmin' in the creek, climbing trees, eatin' muscadines, chasm' junebugs, watchin' tumblebugs, eatin' sour grass, battlin' dead corn stalks, sloppin' hogs, milkin' cows, and readin' in the outhouse.

Now I know you did other things in the outhouse, but readin' the Sears catalog was a main attraction for me. Everybody saved their old catalogs and they wound up in the outhouse for one main purpose and I used them for that, but I also liked to look at the pictures and try to read about things that interested me. Because of this I spent a lot of time in the outhouse just a readin' the Sears catalog. Why, sometimes I would visit it two or three times a day. Word got out that I was the most regular kid around. I did visit the outhouse pretty regular, but most of the time just to read and look at pictures.

Some of my cousins complained that I was using too many pages and that the catalog was not going to last, and then what would they do for paper to you know what with. I'll have to admit I did use a lot of pages 'cause I refused to use half a page, and I also wouldn't use the slick pages. They didn't do a good job.

Sometimes I'd go to the barn and stick some corn cobs in my pocket 'cause they worked better and I wouldn't have to use the catalog pages. This way there would be more pages left to read and more pictures to look at. I tried to get my cousins to use corn cobs, but they wouldn't. They said they didn't have time to run to the barn when nature called. I usually carried a couple of cobs in my pocket, just in case I needed them. It never hurt to be prepared. Besides, a cob in time saves nine catalog pages.

Song: Readin', Rightin', and R'ithmetic

JUST ANY OLE BOTTLE WILL DO!

John Dave (Pete) Fuller

I first started noticing girls in the sixth grade. I had several girlfriends that year, and each one lasted about a week or two, and it was on to the next one. Even though I started noticing girls, I was more interested in art and my sixth grade teacher, Mrs. Cobb, took up a lot of time with me, showing me how to draw. I won several school art contests and Mrs. Cobb wanted me to study art with Kelly Fitzpatrick, an outstanding artist that lived in town, but I never got around to doing that, namely because of the seventh grade.

The seventh grade was totally different from sixth grade. Instead of one teacher who took up a lot of time with each student, there were seven teachers and seven different classes, which lasted about forty-five minutes, and no art classes. I was able to take band classes under Mr. Welch and that satisfied some of my artistic desires, but I still missed art. But it didn't take long for my art desire to disappear because girls began to look more inviting, and now the attraction was stronger, because I got to see older girls since we were in the same building with the high school. Boy, those girls were something else. Course, they paid no attention to me, a lowly seventh grader, but one could daydream and I did a lot of that.

I was larger than the average seventh grader and because of that I was able to associate with a few eight graders, who were more knowledgeable about the opposite sex than me. Because of this I got invited to eight grade parties, but since I didn't live in town I didn't get to go to any since I couldn't drive.

Once my daddy agreed to take me and pick me up at the end of the party. I sure learned a lot at this party about party games, especially spin the bottle, a game I grew to love. At the party everybody would get in a big circle and someone would spin a big bottle. If the neck of the bottle stopped and pointed to you, then the next girl the bottle pointed to after another spin got to take a little walk with you down the street to the corner and back. At first I didn't get it, but one of the older eight grade girls educated me real fast.

On my very first trip down to the corner I was introduced to the kiss. If you don't know what that is I'll explain it to you. It seems a boy put his lips on the lips of a girl. I always thought lips were for eating and talking, but this was better. At first I didn't know what to do when we reached the corner. The girl just stood there with her eyes closed and her lips all puckered up.

After about thirty seconds she opened her eyes, stared at me and said, "Well, are you going to kiss me or not?" I grabbed her hand and kissed it. She said "Not my hand dummy. Kiss me on the lips."

So I did! She wouldn't let me go and at first I wanted to push away. But then it happened. I started getting a tingly feeling all over, especially when she stuck her tongue in between my lips (I later was told this was a French kiss). Then I didn't want to let her go. Well, that was my first kiss that night, but not my last. I couldn't wait for that old bottle to stop on me again.

At school the next day word was out that seventh grader could sure kiss. That old bottle made me a star.

LITTLE GAME HUNTER

John Dave (Pete) Fuller

As a little tyke I had a collection of toy guns. I had a Roy Rodgers cap pistol, a Gene Autry cap pistol, and several no name pistols that only clicked or made some kind of noise. I liked the caps better, 'cause they smoked and sounded loud. I also had a Red Ryder air rifle, but was not allowed BBs to shoot in the gun. I would just pump it up and shoot air.

Us kids would play cowboys and ride our broomstick horses up and down the sidewalks and alleys on our street. I was always Roy Rodgers and my horse was Trigger, but sometimes I had to be the outlaw and rob the bank or highjack the stagecoach. I liked being Roy Rodgers better.

As I got older I graduated from toy cap pistols to sling shots, bows and arrows, and finally a BB gun with real BBs. I mainly hunted birds and occasionally I would see a small rabbit. I never came close to hitting one, let alone killing one.

When I was old enough to be responsible with a gun, my daddy bought me an Iver Johnson single-shot .410 shotgun. I was shown how to load it and told that a gun was always loaded. Never assume a gun is not loaded, 'cause unloaded guns kill people. I was told to never point a gun at anyone and I could only hunt animals for food, such as squirrels and quail.

The 410, with a full choke, was a good squirrel gun and was safer than a rifle since it didn't shoot a great distance, and the shot spread out after 40 or 50 yards, falling harmlessly to the ground. A rifle, however, could kill up to a half a mile away.

I later grew up and learned about rifles and pistols and was taught to always respect guns for what they were used for, to hunt for food, and for protection in the face of danger. I never killed for fun, only for food. I did kill a lot of bottles and cans for fun in order to develop my shooting skills. I've never had to shoot a human being, but would for protection of my family and my life. My guns only do what I make them do.

DRIVER'S EDUCATION

John Dave (Pete) Fuller

One night I had a date with a girl who was a good friend of mine. The only problem was we did not have driver's license, nor a car. We borrowed a car from one of her friends as well as her friend's driver's license. Everything was set, so we thought.

We stayed in our town. I was the driver and everything was fine. We drove around town, talked, and were enjoying our evening. We then stopped and got something to eat before driving across town to take my date home. It would not take long since across town was maybe three or four blocks. We had to cross a fairly long bridge to get to the residential section of town, and everything was going well 'til we got to the end of the bridge. There a car with a red light and a siren appeared. I had to pull over. The officer asked for my driver's license and well, I didn't have one. I had just turned sixteen. I had been driving trucks and tractors since I was twelve, but didn't think it was necessary to tell the officer. About that time my date spoke up.

"Officer. I have my license and I'm helping my friend practice driving."

The officer asked to see the license and my date handed it to him. He flashed his flashlight on us and studied us for several minutes. The officer then asked my date a question.

"Your license shows dark hair, but your hair is blonde. What do you have to say about that?"

"Well officer, how many times do women change their hair color, especially teenagers?"

The officer kept looking at the license and back to my date.

"Well," the officer said, "Everything looks legal. Ya'll be careful and drive safely."

"We will officer," my date and I said in unison.

The officer left and we cranked up and pulled off slowly. He followed us for about a block and passed us, blinking his lights as he passed as if to say, "See you later alligator."

The officer probably remembered his teenage years and maybe did something similar or even worse.

We drove up in my date's driveway and walked to the front door. Did I kiss my date goodnight? You figure it out. I still had to drive my old International truck home, but I made it okay.

HALLOWEEN CARNIVAL

John Dave (Pete) Fuller

This story is true. Only the first names were used to protect the innocent, whoever they were. The guilty know who they are, 'cause they had the most fun.

Well it's October 31 St once again and I can't wait for the Halloween carnival to begin. It's always held in the Old Hohenberg Memorial Elementary School building, built in the thirties. The building was built in a rectangle with a courtyard in the middle and classrooms down each side. The auditorium was in the back, and the front housed the principal's office and some classrooms. A long interior hall formed a large U-shape around the front and up each side. It was a perfect place for a Halloween carnival.

Every classroom had some kind of activity going on in it. There were gofishin' booths, fortune teller booths, haunted house booths, pin-the-tail on the donkey booths, eatin' places, and square and round dancin' in the auditorium. This was a big money maker for the elementary school. Everybody went.

This particular year my current girlfriend, Nancy Ann, was telling fortunes. That meant I didn't do much dancing (Nancy Ann was a good dancer), but spent a lot of time getting my fortune told.

As the night progressed I went through the haunted house and ate a few of the skinned grapes they used for eyeballs, went fishin', bought some popcorn and fudge candy, but didn't try to pin the tail on the donkey. I soon grew bored. My girlfriend had to stay 'til the carnival was over at ten. There was no chance for a date; she had to be home by eleven. What was a teenager to do on Halloween night? No date, but I couldn't go home, not on Halloween night.

Well, I found about fourteen other friends who were bored too. Surely we could find something fun to do. We put our heads together and came up with several fun things to do. Among my friends were

Charles, Dewey, Douglas, Jasper, Truman, Jimmy, Earl, Lewis, and me, Pete. There were others that I can't remember.

First off we jacked up several car rear ends and placed a block under the rear axle so the pulling wheel would not touch the ground. The driver wouldn't notice since the tire was only an inch off the ground. When he cranked the car and put it in gear it would not move. The driver usually gunned it, but it still would not move. Eventually he figured out what was wrong. We didn't stay around for the fun, having other things to do.

We headed for the cotton gin. We decided to push all the cotton bales out in the street to stop traffic. This proved to be disaster for some, namely me, Pete, and Charles, but more about this later. We were having a ball pushing the bales off the platform onto the street, knowing that when the carnival was over this Street would be blocked.

Dewey and I had pushed off several bales and on the fourth bale we heard someone yell. We had pushed one off on Charles. Charles said it only hit him on the leg and it hurt, but he said he would be okay.

After we finished with the bales we lit out for another adventure. We were running down the street and noticed a two-story tin roof house. Who could resist rockin' that tin top house on Halloween night? We proceeded to throw rocks on the house and listen to them roll off, making a terrible loud noise. This was sure to wake up anyone sleeping inside. It did!

Some old geezer ran out on the front porch, raised a double barrel shotgun, and BAM! BAM! Birdshot pellets rained through the trees all above us. Fortunately he shot over us and not at us. We all became instant track stars. I covered several blocks in record time, finally ending up on Charles' front porch. My car was parked at his house.

Charles was laying sprawled on his porch. At first I thought he was just out of breath, but I noticed his right leg was swelled twice the size of his left leg. It seems the cotton bale had broken his leg and he didn't know it at the time, and had run home on a broken leg. I didn't know what to do; neither did Charles. Since Charles was at home I thought his parents could take care of him, so I left and went home.

The next morning at school I was called to the office first thing. Charles had to tell how he broke his leg, confessing that a cotton bale fell on it. Since Charles couldn't push a bale of cotton off the platform on his own leg, someone else had to do it. I was the obvious choice so we both took the rap, not telling on the others.

By lunchtime it was all over school. Pete had pushed a cotton bale on Charles and broken his leg. The weight of the bale started out at 500 pounds, but soon grew to 1,000 pounds, then 1,500 pounds, and finally

2,000 pounds. Nobody ever figured out how I moved that cotton bale by myself.
Song: Ole Man River / Night Riders in the Sky

GRAN-DADDY HICKS AND JAIL TIME

John Dave (Peter) Fuller

Gran-Daddy Hicks was a large man, about six-foot-two and he weighed in at 250 pounds. He had a good crop of hair, which was beginnin' to turn gray. He was not a frail-looking man. He had big bones and not much fat. As some people said he was a stout man. He could lift the back end of a Model-T Ford off the ground and move it. He would demonstrate this feat if you asked him. Course Model T's were scarce in 1941, but could be found.

Gran-Daddy Hicks was a sawmill man in North Carolina up until he moved his family (there were nine children) to Montgomery, Alabama, where he went into the produce business with his son-in-law, Dave Fuller.

Now Montgomery was a wide open town in the 1940s. Plenty of booze, a red-light district, beer parlors abounded (beer joints was the common name), and anything else if you knew the right people.

Gran-Daddy was not a drinkin' man in North Carolina—well, maybe a little nip every now and then—but he picked up the habit in Montgomery. One of his favorite pastimes was to go to the beer parlors and drink after work, or any other convenient time. Occasionally he would drink too much and wind up in a fight, and end up breaking some chairs, bottles, or whatever he could get his hands on. He would usually come home then and try to sleep it off. This worked well unless the barkeep, or whoever Gran-Daddy was fighting (always more than one), decided to press charges. If that happened, it usually meant jail time for Gran-Daddy. Justice was swift in those days: no trial; no jury; just directly to the slammer 'til he sobered up. I can remember vividly what took place when this happened.

The houses on our street were row houses and all had a front porch. I would sit on the porch many an afternoon playing. Gran-Daddy would be in bed trying to sober up. A paddy wagon would drive up and usually about five policemen would get out (remember Gran-Daddy was a big, stout man). I would usually run and tell grandmother the wagon was here, so she could move anything that was breakable out of the way. She would then let the policemen in and they would remove Gran-Daddy. He never went peaceable. It was jail time 'til he sobered up and paid for the damages. You know I bet Gran-Daddy probably paid for redecorating every beer joint in town.

Sometimes the police would call and tell grandma that Gran-Daddy was sober and could come home now. Then about thirty minutes later they would call back and tell us not to come 'cause he was drunk. How could he get drunk in jail? I later found out that one of his daughters would go behind the jail, and Gran-Daddy would hang black thread fishing line out the window. The daughter, Nell Dean, would tie a whiskey bottle on the string and Gran-Daddy would pull it up and get drunk in jail. The jail window was in the alley and nobody ever bothered to check that window.

DELMUS AND THE SIGN POST

John Dave (Pete) Fuller

Delmus and me were brothers and always arguing about who had the best of whatever we had, and who was the best at what we did. My dog could tree more coons than his. His could fight any bobcat or dog in these whereabouts. It went on day in and day out. I could milk a gallon bucket full in a minute or two. Delmus said he could do it with one hand, but I knew he couldn't. But I could have. Those old cow tits are awful slippery when you wet 'em down, and I could pull those tits with the best of 'em.

Every spring we'd get new shoes and Deimus always said his were made better'n mine. I didn't wear mine much anyway, so this didn't bother me.

Our arguing went on constantly. I could drink black coffee fast, but Delmus argued he could do it faster. Nobody owned a clock at our house, so that argument was never settled. On and on we went, day after day, year after year. Then one day I knew Delmus had finally flipped.

I was coming from the back field and as I topped a little knoll I heard Delmus arguing with someone, but I couldn't hear or see the other person. I listened carefully as I quickly hid, hoping to slip up on Delmus and whoever he was arguing with. They seemed to be arguing about how far it was to Flea Hop, a little community up the ways a bit.

"I don't care what you say," I'd hear Delmus say. "I know Flea Hop ain't but seven miles up the road and you say it's nine. You are wrong! Dead wrong! I have walked it many a time and I know it's only seven miles. I don't care what you say."

Boy did he sound determined, but I still couldn't hear who Delmus was arguing with. He must have been talking real low. I crawled up to the top of the knoll, still hid in the tall grass, to get a better look. Why, I couldn't believe my eyeballs. There stood Delmus by the side of the road staring dead ahead and talking to a sign post that had "Flea Hop 9 Miles" written on it.

"It's only seven miles," Delmus kept sayin'.

Yep. There was Delmus, big as Ike, arguing with a sign post. I never did figure out who was right.

SNAKIN' LOGS

John Dave (Pete) Fuller

Ole Joe didn't want to get out in the cold weather either, but some logs had to be snaked out of the woods for firewood, so I hitched Joe up and headed for the woods. The sun was higher now and you could feel its warmth as me and Joe got closer to our destination.

I could see the logs now. Guess there were about seven or eight of them. It'd probably take me and Joe half a day to snake them to the house.

I backed Joe up to the first log we came to and began to clear the dead brush away. These logs had been cut in early fall and a place had to be cleaned out to put the chain under the log. I had to lay down next to the log to slip the chain under it to the other side. There it was, all the way L) under. I hooked it on top and then hitched it to the trace hangin' on Joe. "Git up," I yelled at Joe, and he started to pull and the log began to move. The log was not large so Joe was doing pretty good.

As the log slid out of its resting place I noticed something under the log right where I had slid the chain under the log. "Whoa," I yelled at Joe and he stopped. I took a closer look. SNAKES alive, there lay the biggest rattlesnake I had seen in a long time. He wasn't moving fast though. I guess the cold weather had slowed him down a bit. I picked him up by the back of the head and threw him out of the way. He was so slowed by the cold he didn't know I was in the world. Sure couldn't have done that in the summertime. He'd bit the daylights outta me. I checked the next log real careful before I slid the chain under it, not that I was scared of snakes, I just didn't like to lay down next to one.

I hitched old Joe up to the next log and got back to the chore of snakin' logs.

"Gee Mule! I mean Haw!"

Never could remember which was which. Sure glad the mule did though.

TRICK AND NO TREAT

John Dave (Pete) Fuller

There's not a lot to do in the country at night. Usually everybody goes to bed at sunset or sometime after, but not on Halloween night. If you are young and looking for some devilment to get into, what better time than with all the other ghosts and goblins? I didn't believe in spooks, but fun was fun, and spooks or no spooks, I was goin' to have some fun on Halloween night.

As soon as it was dark I slipped out of my bedroom window and headed for the crossroads, knowing that Delmus (my brother) and some other fellas would be waitin' for me. I always was the cat's tail. They were waitin' on me alright, and raring to go.

Who would we play a trick on first? We decided it would be *Ole Man Mose*. It had been a long time since we tricked him. Tonight we decided to move his outhouse, but instead of moving it to the woods like we did last time, we moved it back just behind the hole. Delmus almost fell in the hole, but the five of us got it moved and covered up the hole with some tree limbs and dead leaves. The hole wasn't very wide, just wide enough and deep enough *for Ole Man Mose* to fit into with about a foot or two left over. We didn't wait around to see if he fell in, figuring we'd hear about it anyway. We had a lot of tricking to do before midnight.

Who would be next? Why not play a trick on the new school teacher and her husband. They had only been in the community for a few months. They had moved up from Greenville. He was a preacher and was called to preach in our little community of Friendship. I don't know who called him, but I bet after 'bout a year somebody calls him somewhere else. Preachers don't stay here very long. I don't know why.

Anyway, we decided to play the old bag trick on him. Delmus ran out in the cow pasture with a paper bag and scooped up the freshest pile of cow shit he could find in the bag and tied the top with a piece of string. Cow's is better than horse's cause its mushier.

I slipped up to the front door and laid the sack down, took out a match and lit the edge of the sack, making sure it caught good. Then I knocked loudly on the door and ran back to the others, who were hiding at the edge of the yard in the hedge row.

"I hope he heard you," Delmus said in a low voice, cause the sack was beginning to burn real good.

Just then Brother Jones opened the door. We could see him real good cause the sack was lit up good by now. Brother Jones took one look at the burning sack and begin to try to stomp it out with his foot. Gosh, what a mess he made. He got the fire put out, but seemed to be muttering in an unknown tongue. It sounded like *ZX!'><XXZZ COW-SHEET* and *HELL-FAR*, as far as I could make out.

We left running and laughing so hard I ran smack over Delmus, who was bent over double from laughing. I'll bet he'll never get those shoed clean. I hope he had on shoes.

Song: Night Riders in the Sky

ADDITIONAL WRITINGS
John Dave (Pete) Fuller

ABOVE THE BRIGHT BLUE

John Dave (Pete) Fuller

A dream about a country village found while driving in the backwoods. Primitive people lived there. Some old with ailments, some young, some middle age. Story begins with a young woman walking down a country road singing above song (Above the Bright Blue). After hearing her sing, she disappeared down the road. I searched 'til I finally found the village. There were people there who worked hard and everyone had problems (old man with the shakes). Chuck (Wells) a country singer looking for "A Wonderful Place Called Heaven".

DIBBLE DABBLE

John Dave (Pete) Fuller

This was a game we played at the swimming hole. We'd take a matchstick and someone would take it to the bottom, and quickly jump back on the bank. Everybody would look for the matchstick, and if you saw it first you would yell "Dibble Dabble" and jump in and try to grab the stick. Course there were three or four other guys trying to get the stick also, and a lot of battling went on 'til someone grabbed the stick. That person got to take it to the bottom the next time. The game was usually played 'til everybody got waterlogged.

WATER TAG

John Dave (Pete) Fuller

This was played like regular tag except in the water. You had to be a fast swimmer or you stayed "It" most of the time. You could get out of the water and run on the bank, or swim under the water. This game made you develop your swimming skills.

"In the line of fire"

ELIZABETH AND BUTCH

(Describe them later in the story)

I first met Elizabeth and Butch in Calera, Alabama, where I was trying out for the preaching position. Elizabeth was a widow and Butch was her retarded son.

Adopted in 1939 when three days old, the day was the 22nd, 23rd, or 24th. I was born the 24th by Dave and Ecie Fuller. My given name on the birth certificate was John Dave Fuller. The nickname "Pete" was given later.

I was conceived in sin, probably in the month of May. My mother was named Madge Henry. My father remains unknown. He was a high school music teacher. Kind of reminds you of *76 Trombones without the kid*, doesn't it?

I respect Madge Henry because of what she did for me. Being born a bastard in 1939 did not guarantee an Oscar. She found me a legal mother and father. Besides, she grew up in a large family and at a time a bastard was looked down on, even if he did learn to play a trombone (fair), trumpet, French horn, alto sax, clarinet and flute (you've got to be kidding). Truman Welch would have a good laugh on that one. I did major in Music Ed. at Auburn University. I studied voice under Craig Hankenson, an outstanding voice teacher.

Well, I started the *In The Line Of Fire* in 1939.

I would like for this story to be about all the people who helped me *In The Line Of Fire*.

DAVE AND ECIE FULLER
"The Starting Line"
My dad let me sleep with him 'til I was five.

MY TERRITORY AS A FOUR-YEAR-OLD

John Dave (Pete) Fuller

The year was 1943. I was four-years-old. My dad owned a produce company and gas station on Madison Avenue next to the Episcopal church. The church was on one corner and my dad's Texaco station was on the other corner. The produce lot was in the middle.

The Sheridan Hotel was across the street from the Episcopal church, on the corner across from the City Auditorium and City Hall.

Behind the Episcopal church was the Coca Cola Bottling Company. This completed one block. Next to Coca Cola was Mrs. Sheehan's large stone house with a large patio and an efficiency apartment, which she rented out. I later found out, after I was grown and married in 1958, that my future mother-in-law, Margaret Beverett, lived here with Jim Beverett, my future father-in-law. This completed one block.

Beginning on Lawrence Street was the front of Mrs. Sheehan's house. Next to Mrs. Sheehan's house were three or four two-story project houses. My grandparents, Gracie and Dad Hicks, lived in one on the first floor, and my parents, Dave and Ecie Fuller, lived upstairs. Don Garner and his parents lived in one of the others. Don and his sisters were playmates of mine. Don and I would later cross paths in the 1950s in Elmore County. He went to Holtville High School and I went to Wetumpka High School.

My grandad, Dad "By Jacks" Hicks, completed this block on Lawrence Street.

READIN' MATERIAL

John Dave (Pete) Fuller

Outdoor toilets were common in the country when I was growing up. The Sears and Roebuck catalog provided reading material while you were sitting on the toilet and provided other material when you got ready to get up. Those catalogs were valuable.

GAMBLIN' GAME
John Dave (Pete) Fuller

Young boys livin' in the country had to create our fun, since toys were scarce, so we made up games to play. One fun game we played in the summer was *Who's the Fastest*. We would find a wasp nest, the bigger the better, and all line up under the nest. Someone would count to three and hit the nest with a stick. The one who got the furthest away from the nest before they got stung was the winner, and the fastest.

THE CONCEPTION AND EARLY LIFE OF JOHN DAVID FULLER, JR., ALIAS "PETE"

John Dave (Pete) Fuller

As an adult I was asked by someone why I was a member of the *Church of Christ*. I answered their question by telling them that I was born in Montgomery, Alabama, on January 22nd, 23rd, or 24th, 1939, and delivered by a Dr. Black. I was conceived in sin.

My mother was a high school student and my father was a teacher at my mother's school. My mother chose to come to Montgomery to have me, since illegitimate children were considered as "bastards" and people would talk in her hometown. She chose to give me away to a legitimate couple so that nobody would know the real story. Her home and school were in L.A. (that's Lower Alabama for all of you uninformed people). Now, Lower Alabama has many towns and schools, so be my guest and guess which one.

I was adopted by Dave and Ecie Fuller. My father owned a filling station and produce market in Montgomery, so my early years were spent in Montgomery on Madison Avenue and Lawrence Street.

Many people have asked me where the nickname "Pete" came from. I have kept this a secret for the past seventy-five years. There have been many guesses: an uncle, aunt, friend, dog, cow, pig, peat moss, the apostle Peter, and a male sex organ (give me a break), or just petered out. Send me a hundred dollar bill and I will tell you. Just kidding.

Well, since seventy-five years have passed I guess I will let the cat out of the bag. My dad was a successful businessman all of his life, but he could not read very well nor write very well. His favorite joke was that he only went to school three days and that was in his brother's place. My dad did go to school in a one-room schoolhouse close to Friendship, Alabama.

My dad liked Western movies and he told me he nicknamed me "Pete" after one of the outlaws in one of the movies. I was glad he did. I never did like being called John David in elementary school, so I registered under the name of "Pete" when I entered junior high and high school. It took the school administration seven months to find out where John David had disappeared to.

My parents raised me well. I only received one whipping from my dad and that was for coming home riding my bicycle at dusk. My dad took me to the movies after he whipped me, and yes, it was a Western movie. It only cost me a dime to get in, and for a quarter you could buy a bag of popcorn and a cold drink. My dad sat about halfway down and I would sit on the front row where you felt like you were in the movie.

A favorite game I would play was trying to shoot the outlaws. I would make up a bunch of spitballs and put them in a bag to take in with me. After borrowing a quarter for a drink and popcorn, I would ask for an extra straw or two. They made good play guns to shoot spitballs at the outlaws. When you put a spitball in a straw and blew on one end the ball would be launched at the screen. It looked like a small meteor flying through space. You could get away with this if you only shot one spitball at a time. If you shot too many an usher would come looking and you would have to hide your spitballs. I never got caught since I only shot at the bad men. Now you know the rest of the story.

THE SWEETGUM TREE GAME

John Dave (Pete) Fuller

In the south sweetgum trees are everywhere. One of our favorite games was to find a small sweetgum tree, about four to five inches in diameter, about fifteen to twenty feet tall (the higher the better) and climb to the top. You would then start the tree swaying back and forth, and hold on for dear life, and ride it to the ground. It was a smooth fun ride if the tree didn't break. If the tree broke you came down like a rock.

SHOOTIN' SNIPE

John Dave (Pete) Fuller

When I was ten my daddy bought me an Iver Johnson .410 single shotgun. After school I couldn't wait for the school bus to get me home. I'd run and get my shotgun and my daddy would give me one shell only each afternoon. I would go down to a low wetland area in a field to look for snipe, a long-billed, long-necked bird that could fly like a bullet. They would fly straight up off the ground and frop one little turd and zip, they would be gone. If you didn't hit 'em before they dropped the turd, you wouldn't hit 'em. If you did it was pure luck. I wasted many a shell on those snipe before I learned to hit 'em. Then it was no fun anymore.

THIS IS YOUR LIFE

John Dave (Pete) Fuller

In the year 1945 I had just turned six and was looking forward to starting to school in September. I didn't know what school was, but for some strange reason I was real excited about getting to go to school.

About one month before school started my mother took me to town and bought me some school clothes. I was all set for the first day of school. I was nervous all the way from my house to the schoolhouse in Wetumpka, Alabama. The name of the school was Hohenburg Memorial, a red brick budding with a double door in the middle, and two single doors on each end. The floors were wooden and oiled. There were children and parents everywhere.

My mother and I made our way with everybody else to the auditorium and we all took a seat. A man got up and introduced himself. He said he was the principal and his name was Mr. Waldrip. He then introduced all the teachers. There were three first grade teachers: Mrs. Daniel, Mrs. Kelley, and Mrs. Melton. My teacher was to be Mrs. Kelley. She was a nice-looking lady with silver hair and dressed very neat.

We eventually made it to our classroom, which was decorated with all kinds of colorful things, a playhouse in one corner, tables and chairs, and a place to take a nap after lunch. Well, our first day was over at 12 o'clock and my mother and I went home. I was looking forward for the first full day, because I was going to get to ride a yellow school bus.

My first full day was filled with fun things to do. We got to draw pictures, play games, take a nap after lunch, listen to stories told by Mrs. Melton, and learn to read and write. My first year went by real fast, as did my next five years. Then on to my next six, and finally graduating in 1957. School life in the fifties was very relaxed.

There were two tracks to travel on through high school. There was college prep for those who planned to go to college, and a track for those who wanted to learn about business, or become a farmer and raise cattle, or learn any trade. There were certain classes designed for anyone, including the arts, such as band, glee club, and voice. I don't think there was an actual class to learn to draw, although I did study art in the sixth grade.

My sixth grade teacher, Mrs. Cobb, was a very fine artist. She encouraged me to continue my art and to study with Mr. Kelly Fitzpatrick, but for some reason I did not. I did go on to college and earn a B.S. in music. I studied vocal and instrumental music and became a choral and band director.

I think I received a good education and upon graduation from college I started teaching in 1963. My first teaching job was Maxwell Elementary on Maxwell Air Force Base. This was the first integrated school in Alabama. The school was built on the airbase right across the street from Pendar Street Elementary. A fence separated the two schools.

My first year of teaching was eventful. I taught sixteen classes a day of general music and chorus. There were three sections of grades 1 through 4, and two sections of grades 5 and 6. The first through fourth grade classes were 20 minutes long and the fifth and sixth grade classes were 30 minutes long. I ate lunch between the 4th and 5th grade classes.

I directed a Christmas program using my fourth, fifth and sixth graders. I arranged the music for a small string ensemble and a chorus comprised of my students. The ensemble was made up of students from the Montgomery Youth Symphony. It was a wonderful concert. The response was great and we had two performances to accommodate the parents on two different nights. You might recall that John F. Kennedy was assassinated in the fall of 1963, so the first semester was very tense at the school. I think maybe our concert eased the tension somewhat.

Teaching sixteen periods a day must have gotten to me however, for one day in January I began to feel dizzy and went to the teacher's lounge, which was next to my classroom. I threw up in the bathroom and immediately felt better. I sat down and drank a coke and went back and finished the day. I went home and began to feel dizzy again, but ate a supper of spaghetti and meatballs, and stayed up late to watch a movie on our T.V. starring Paul Newman and Liz Taylor entitled *Cat on a Hot Tin Roof*. Several times during the movie I would run to the bathroom and throw up. The color was brownish red. The meatballs were coming back up I thought. About two in the morning I finally went to bed.

I woke up about six o'clock, went in the bathroom, and threw up one last time. I then took a bath and shaved, and was feeling great. I put my clothes on, went to the bathroom door, reached above the doorjam to stretch, and told my wife Charlotte I was feeling great. The next thing I remembered was sitting slumped over on the passenger side of the car with my head out the window. I felt great. The wind felt so cool on my skin. They were rushing me to the hospital.

When I arrived the doctor took one look at me and started giving me blood in both arms. They didn't take time to warm the blood, so they wrapped me in blankets to keep me warm. It was touch and go for about a week. I was in and out of consciousness. I was later told that when I arrived at the hospital I didn't have but about a pint of blood left in my body. The doctor didn't think I was going to make it. I had been bleeding internally for two days and had thrown up most of my blood. One more bad throw up and I would have died the doctor said.

They kept giving me blood and after a week I stopped bleeding and began to improve. I did finish the school year, but choose to leave elementary teaching, and took a band job in Carbon Hill, Alabama, in June of 1964.

ABORTED
Pete Fuller

Oh Mother dear,
Why didn't you keep me?
Why couldn't you see what I was going to be?

Oh Mother dear,
Why, why didn't you believe?
Why didn't you know how much I'd love you so?

My first breath never came;
I never got the chance
To laugh at silly little things,
Or play in the rain.

You never experienced the joy or the laughter
That an innocent child can give,
Because you just didn't have the courage
To say, "I'll have faith and let it live."

I wasn't there to care for you,
And to take care of you in your old age.

OH SWEET BUTTERFLY
Pete Fuller

Oh sweet butterfly,
You float so sweetly in the sky
With your wings spread wide.
You just glide and glide.

Oh sweet butterfly
You make me cry.
Why did you fly away?

PICTURE REFERENCES

John Dave "Pete" Fuller, Jr.

Ecie Alberta Hicks Fuller, Pete's Mother
Daughters, Jerry Sue and Diana Loree

Dance Hall. Pete's Parents Owned.

John Dave "Pete" Fuller, Jr.
John Dave Fuller, Sr.

Dr. Pepper Truck Pete drove. 1958 and 1959.

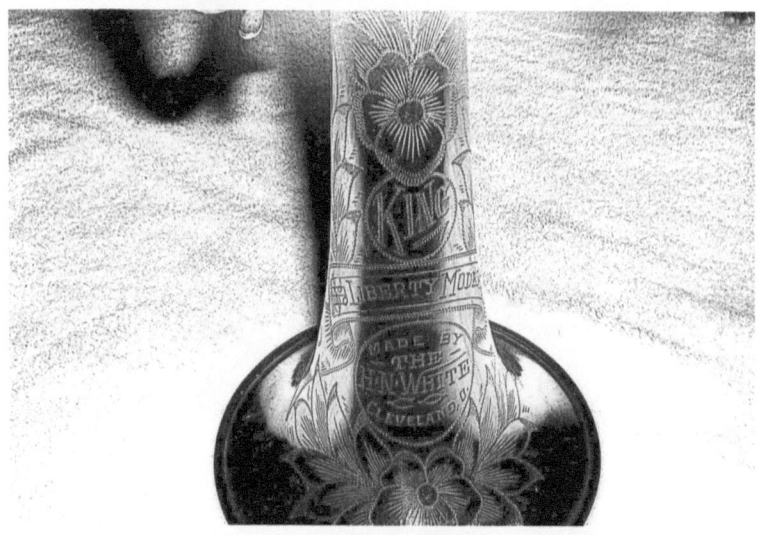

Pete's Trumpet

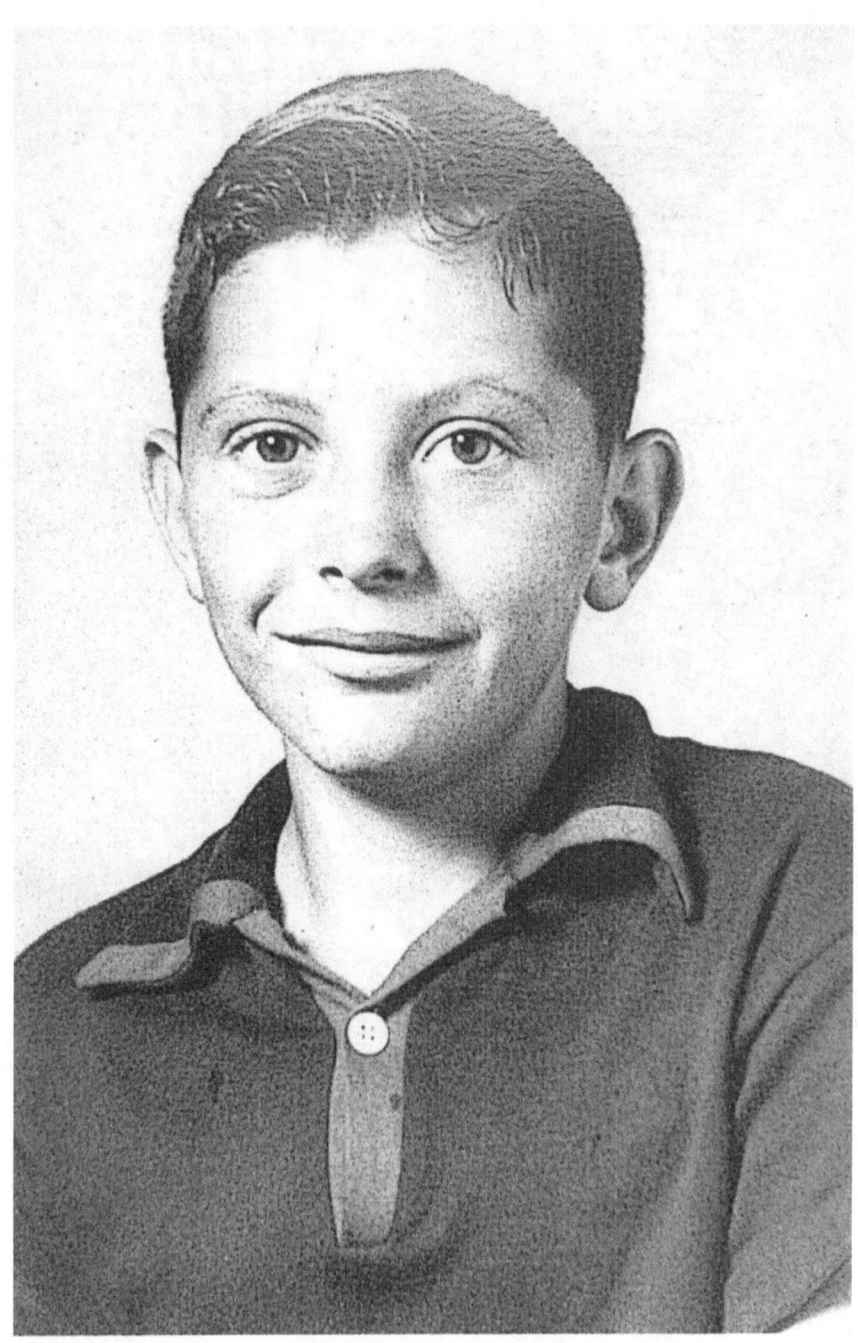

John Dave "Pete" Fuller, Jr.

Charlotte Ann Beverett Fuller
John Dave "Pete" Fuller, Jr.
Diana Loree Fuller
Jerry Sue Fuller

www.ingramcontent.com/pod-product-compliance
Lightning Source LLC
LaVergne TN
LVHW091600060526
838200LV00036B/926